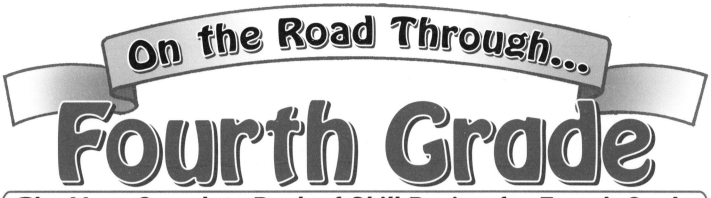

On the Road Through...
Fourth Grade

The Most Complete Book of Skill Review for Fourth Grade

Adapted by
Sherrill B. Flora

Mini-Books by
Wolfgang Hoelscher

Cover Design and Illustrations by
Dan Sharp

D1307273

Publisher
Carson-Dellosa Publishing Company, Inc.
Greensboro, North Carolina

Credits

Authors	Sherrill B. Flora, Wolfgang Hoelscher
Editors	Kelly Morris Huxmann, Debra Olson Pressnall
Art Direction	Annette Hollister-Papp
Cover Design and Illustrations	Dan Sharp
Graphic Layout	Gray House Graphics, Mark Conrad

CD-0320   ISBN 0-88724-753-9

Table of Contents

Table of Contents

Contents by Skill

Contents by Skill

Introduction

Dear Parent,

Welcome to *On the Road through Fourth Grade*. Fourth grade often marks the end of elementary school. At this age, children are maturing, able to set standards for themselves, and developing personal interests and talents. Fourth graders are learning to use their academic skills as life skills. They are reading for knowledge and enjoyment, using real-world math skills and discovering an increased ability to communicate through the written word.

For some children, fourth grade also marks the emergence of the preteen. This can mean that you might begin to see moodiness and some rebellious behaviors in your child. Children at this age are trying to grow up and become more independent. As parents, we want our children to think independently and to act critically and responsibly. To accomplish this, children need to put some distance between themselves and their parents. Do not let this distancing behavior alarm you. Instead, try to understand it and keep the lines of communication open. Encourage sharing. Ask questions. Be ready to listen.

Your emerging preteen also needs to be surrounded by a positive environment. Instead of constantly reminding her to complete tasks or reprimanding her when you think she is wrong, try finding moments throughout the day when you say only positive comments to your child. Your child needs your support and encouragement now, even more than when she was little. Provide a home and atmosphere that will promote open and honest communication.

Friends are becoming increasingly more important. Your child is developing social skills and is now able to engage in group decision-making. You will also find that many fourth graders have developed a great sense of truthfulness—they can be incredibly honest. This is a trait that we want to last forever!

Fourth grade children are getting ready to take that leap into more abstract thinking. For this reason, it is vital that children have developed a solid foundation of basic skills. The skill review provided in *On the Road through Fourth Grade* helps strengthen that foundation for further school success—and it is fun!

Language Arts

The single most important skill that a child needs for success in school, and later in life, is to be "literate." In other words, your child must learn how to read. You can do many things to encourage literacy.

- Encourage your child to read every day, whether it be books, magazines, short stories, or poetry.
- Read the same books your child is reading so you can share the stories together. Talk about what is going to happen next, have your child make up a new ending for the story, and discuss the characters, plot, and setting.
- Go to the library and let your child choose new books.
- Write a story together. Have your child illustrate the story.
- Have your child make a comic book.
- Fill your child's environment with literacy materials like books, magazines, newspapers, catalogs, paper, pencils, crayons, paints, and music CDs.
- Encourage your child to write thank-you notes or letters.
- Together make a scrapbook of fourth-grade memories.
- Supervise your child's use of the Internet. Search for stories, games, and learning activities that your child can enjoy on-line. (See Web sites, page 9.)
- Take your child to a play or some type of theatrical production.
- Encourage your child to read and write poetry.
- Ask your child to look through the newspaper for information: weather, sports, local events, national news, comics, and movie listings.
- Have your child make her own address and phone directory.

Math and Science

So many toys and puzzles provide children with early math and science learning experiences. Remember to point out all the ways we use numbers and science in our daily lives. Here are some suggested materials and activities:

- Get your child a watch and encourage telling time and being on time.
- Provide blocks, puzzles, and other building materials.
- Encourage play with magnets, scales, and science books and kits.
- Have your child practice using numbers "in his head" (mental math).
- Help your child learn basic math facts. Play math games. (See Web sites, page 9.)
- Play card games. This can help children learn to add quickly.
- Play games with your child. Trivia, word, math, and problem-solving games can make for a fun family evening.
- Visit science, art, and history museums.
- Discuss how we use numbers in the real world.
- Encourage your child to begin a hobby. Encourage individual interests.
- Encourage an interest in music.

Fun Web Sites for Fourth Graders

http://www.bookadventure.org/ki/index.asp

The "Book Finder" helps kids find books at a particular reading level and on specific topics chosen by the child. Some site features require free registration.

http://www.childrensmuseum.org/funonline/funonline.html

At this interactive site, kids can learn about living in space, create a multimedia project, solve science mysteries, and play on-line games. The Children's Museum of Indianapolis maintains this Web site.

http://www.coolmath4kids.com

This colorful site offers interactive math games, puzzles, math tricks, and calculators. Topics include whole number operations, tessellations, fractions, geometry, logic problems, algebra, and probability. At this fun site, kids can practice math skills and learn about fascinating math concepts.

http://www.factmonster.com

Lots and lots of facts are offered at this Web site. Visitors can learn about countries and people, the United States, math concepts, sports, and science topics such as stars and planets, weather, animals, and the human body. Interactive educational games as well as arcade games and a homework center are included.

http://funbrain.com/kidscenter.html

Site features a variety of interactive games with multiple skill levels that cover math, language arts, and science concepts. Visitors can practice math facts, rounding numbers and identifying place value, reading comprehension and spelling skills, and much more.

http://www.kidshealth.org/kid/

At this site, kids can read about dealing with feelings in different situations, find out about caring for their bodies to stay healthy, and take an interactive tour of the systems of the body. Other health topics are included. A search can be done for specific questions.

http://www.kidskonnect.com

This safe Internet gateway for kids offers an extensive list of links to informative Web sites. Categories include animals, countries, games and puzzles, geography, health, holidays and seasons, language arts, math, museums, music, people, sports, states, transportation, and others.

http://www.missmaggie.org

Animated stories and interactive games introduce kids to real-life environmental problems at this Web site. As kids complete each Earth Adventure mission, they apply math, science, language arts and problem-solving skills.

http://www.nasa.gov/kids.html

This site is sponsored by NASA and offers puzzles, games, and science stories. Kids can learn about the space shuttle, rockets and airplanes, the Space Station, stars, and much more. Fun project ideas and activities are included.

http://www.nationalgeographic.com/kids/

Site includes fun facts, coloring pages, games, homework help, and maps. Also provides a link to the on-line edition of *National Geographic for Kids*.

http://www.ology.amnh.org/index.html

This interactive site will introduce kids to dinosaurs and fossils, the planets and the Milky Way, and other science topics. Kids are encouraged to collect "Ology" cards that feature fun facts, learn about the work of a paleontologist and an astronomer, read stories, solve puzzles, and play games. The site is maintained by the American Museum of Natural History in New York City.

http://www.thunk.com

At this fun Web site, kids can change their words into secret messages for friends to unscramble. Links to FBI for Kids, CIA for Kids, and science Web sites are provided.

http://www.urbanext.uiuc.edu/kids/index.html

Site features interactive activities about planning and caring for a garden, how foods grow, earthworms, and getting along with people. Kids can play games, read short stories, and learn interesting facts to understand the mysteries of plant life and the importance of earthworms.

http://www.wordcentral.com

Learning new words can be fun. At this site, kids find out about new words by reading the "Daily Buzzword," discover how words get into the dictionary, and look up words to find out their meanings. This site is maintained by Merriam-Webster.

Recommended Books for Fourth Graders

A

The Adventures of Pippi Longstocking by Astrid
  Lindgren
Alien Alert by Susan Korman
Annie and the Old One by Miska Miles
Attaboy, Sam! by Lois Lowry

B

The BFG by Roald Dahl
Babe: The Gallant Pig by Dick King-Smith
Basil of Baker Street by Eve Titus
The Black Stallion by Walter Farley
The Black Stallion and Flame by Walter Farley
The Black Stallion and the Girl by Walter Farley
The Black Stallion Challenged by Walter Farley
The Black Stallion Returns by Walter Farley
The Borrowers by Mary Norton
The Boxcar Children by Gertrude Chandler
  Warner

C

Caddie Woodlawn by Carol Ryrie Brink
Charlie and the Chocolate Factory
  by Roald Dahl
Charlie and the Great Glass Elevator
  by Roald Dahl
Chocolate-Covered Ants by Stephen Manes
Cricket and the Crackerbox Kid
  by Alane Ferguson

D

Dinotopia: A Land Apart from Time
  by James Gurney
Dunc and Amos Hit the Big Top
  by Gary Paulsen
Dunc's Doll by Gary Paulsen

E

Emily's Runaway Imagination by Beverly Cleary

F

Fantastic Mr. Fox by Roald Dahl
Finding the Titanic by Robert D. Ballard
For the Love of Peanuts by Charles M. Schulz
*For Laughing Out Loud: Poems to Tickle Your
  Funnybone*, selected by Jack Prelutsky
Fourth-Grade Celebrity by Patricia Reilly Giff

Fourth Graders Don't Believe in Witches
  by Terri Fields
The Fox Busters by Dick King-Smith
Fudge-a-Mania by Judy Blume

G

Gentle Ben by Walt Morey
George's Marvelous Medicine by Roald Dahl
The Ghost of Popcorn Hill by Betty Ren Wright
Good-Bye, My Wishing Star by Vicki Grove
Goodbye, Vietnam by Gloria Whelan
A Grain of Rice by Helena Clare Pittman
The Great Brain by John D. Fitzgerald
The Great Brain at the Academy
  by John D. Fitzgerald
The Great Brain Does It Again
  by John D. Fitzgerald
The Great Brain Reforms by John D. Fitzgerald

H

Hardy Boys: The Bombay Boomerang
  by Franklin W. Dixon
Hardy Boys: Hunting for Hidden Gold
  by Franklin W. Dixon
Hardy Boys: The Mystery of Smugglers Cove
  by Franklin W. Dixon
Hardy Boys: The Secret of the Old Mill
  by Franklin W. Dixon
Hardy Boys: The Shattered Helmet
  by Franklin W. Dixon
Hatchet by Gary Paulsen
Help! I'm a Prisoner in the Library by Eth Clifford
Henry Huggins by Beverly Cleary
How to Eat Fried Worms by Thomas Rockwell
The Hundred Dresses by Eleanor Estes

I

Iggie's House by Judy Blume
Incognito Mosquito Flies Again by E. A. Hass
Incognito Mosquito, Private Insective
  by E. A. Hass

J

Jacob Two-Two and the Dinosaur
  by Mordecai Richler
Jacob Two-Two Meets the Hooded Fang
  by Mordecai Richler
Just So Stories by Rudyard Kipling

L

A Light in the Attic by Shel Silverstein
Little House in the Big Woods
    by Laura Ingalls Wilder
Lon Po Po: A Red-Riding Hood Story from
    China by Ed Young

M

The Magic School Bus at the Waterworks
    by Joanna Cole
The Magic School Bus: Gets Baked in a Cake
    by Joanna Cole
The Magic School Bus: Inside the Earth
    by Joanna Cole
The Magic School Bus: Inside the Human Body
    by Joanna Cole
The Magic School Bus: Lost in the Solar System
    by Joanna Cole
Make Four Million Dollars by Next Thursday
    by Stephen Manes
Matilda by Roald Dahl
Matthew Jackson Meets the Wall by Patricia
    Reilly Giff
Mitch and Amy by Beverly Cleary
More Adventures of the Great Brain
    by John D. Fitzgerald
The Mouse and the Motorcycle
    by Beverly Cleary
Mr. Popper's Penguins by Richard Atwater
My Teacher Is an Alien by Bruce Coville

N

Nancy Drew Mysteries: The Case of the
    Disappearing Diamonds by Carolyn Keene
Nancy Drew Mysteries: The Clue in the
    Crumbling Wall by Carolyn Keene
Nancy Drew Mysteries: The Double Jinx Mystery
    by Carolyn Keene
Nancy Drew Mysteries: The Ghost of
    Blackwood Hall by Carolyn Keene
Nancy Drew Mysteries: The Secret in the Old
    Attic by Carolyn Keene

O

ORP by Suzy Kline
Orp and the Chop Suey Burgers by Suzy Kline
Orp Goes to the Hoop by Suzy Kline

Otis Spofford by Beverly Cleary
Owls in the Family by Farley Mowat

P

Paul Bunyan by Steven Kellogg
Poison Ivy and Eyebrow Wigs by Bonnie Pryor

R

Rabbit Hill by Robert Lawson
The Rag Coat by Lauren A. Mills
The Reluctant Dragon by Kenneth Grahame
The Return of the Great Brain by John D.
    Fitzgerald
Rodomonte's Revenge by Gary Paulsen

S

Sarah, Plain and Tall by Patricia MacLachlan
Shiloh by Phyllis Reynolds Naylor
Sideways Arithmetic from Wayside School
    by Louis Sachar
Sideways Stories from Wayside School
    by Louis Sachar
Snow Treasure by Marie McSwigan
Socks by Beverly Cleary
Squanto, Friend of the Pilgrims
    by Clyde Robert Bulla
Stepbrother Sabotage by Sally Wittman
Stone Fox by John Reynolds Gardiner
Strawberry Girl by Lois Lenski
Strider by Beverly Cleary
Superfudge by Judy Blume

T

Tales of a Fourth Grade Nothing by Judy Blume
There's a Boy in the Girls' Bathroom
    by Louis Sachar

V

The Velveteen Rabbit by Margery Williams

W

Where the Sidewalk Ends by Shel Silverstein
The Whipping Boy by Sid Fleischman
Who's Orp's Girlfriend? by Suzy Kline
The Wild Culpepper Cruise by Gary Paulsen

Fourth Grade Skills Checklist

This list is an overview of some of the key skills learned in fourth grade. When using this list, please keep in mind that the curriculum will vary across the United States, as will how much an individual teacher is able to teach over the course of one year. The list will give you an overview of the majority of fourth grade skills and assist you in motivating, guiding, and helping your child maintain or even increase skills.

Language Arts/Reading

Is able to complete analogies .... ❏

Recognizes compound words.. ❏

Recognizes contractions.. ❏

Recognizes antonyms, synonyms, and homonyms .... ❏

Recognizes tenses of verbs.. ❏

Recognizes parts of speech .... ❏

Uses correct punuctuation .... ❏

Recognizes complete and incomplete sentences .... ❏

Uses possessives properly .... ❏

Can identity the main idea from context clues in a story .... ❏

Can identify the setting of a story .... ❏

Can identify the conflict of a story .... ❏

Can identify the conclusion of a story .... ❏

Can identify cause and effect relationships of a story .... ❏

Can make preditions from content clues.. ❏

Can identify common abbrevations.. ❏

Uses correctly the writing and editing process .... ❏

Can use a dictionary, thesaurus, and encyclopedia .... ❏

Can identify prefixes and suffixes.. ❏

Is able to construct a short story .... ❏

Is able to write a friendly letter, business letter, invitation .... ❏

Reads and writes for pleasure.. ❏

Recognizes literatures genres: poetry, nonfiction, tall tales, etc. .... ❏

Math

Recognizes numbers to 9,999,999 ....❏

Can identify two- and three-dimentional geometric shapes ....❏

Can interpret and read a graph ....❏

Understands place value up to the millions place.................................❏

Is able to use decimals to the hundredth place ....❏

Can recall all addition facts (sums to 24) ....❏

Can recall all subtraction facts (subtrahends: 0–10)............................❏

Can recall all multiplication facts (factors: 0–12) ....❏

Can recall all division facts (divisors: 1–9) ....❏

Can perform multiplication word problems, 2-digits times 3-digits ....❏

Can perform division word problems with 2-digit divisors ....❏

Performs four-digit addition, with regrouping ....❏

Performs four-digit subtraction, with regrouping ....❏

Can make estimations ....❏

Knows the value of money combinations..❏

Can count money using coins in combination ....❏

Can count money to make change ....❏

Can perform money addition and subtraction problems
using a decimal point ....❏

Can tell time by the minute ....❏

Can measure using standard units ....❏

Can measure using the metric system...❏

Can order fractions ....❏

Can add and subtract mixed whole numbers ....❏

Can find equivalent fractions ....❏

Uses problem-solving strategies to complete math problems ....❏

Cursive Letter Practice

Trace and write the cursive letters.

Aa Bb Cc

Dd Ee Ff

Gg Hh Ii

Jj Kk Ll

Mm Nn

Oo Pp Qq

Rr Ss Tt

Uu Vv Ww

Xx Yy Zz

Cursive Writing Evaluation

Copy the poem in your best cursive handwriting.

There was a rabbit

With a bad habit

Of jumping on places

Like crocodiles' faces!

15

Matching Vowel Sounds

Draw a line to connect each word in the first column with a word in the second column that has the **same vowel sound**.

ax	big
cool	cat
cup	led
egg	pay
lake	school
like	smile
lit	toll
load	up

Identifying Place Value

Write the **place value** of the highlighted digit on the line.
The first one has been done for you.

A. 8,567,123 _____ten thousands_____

B. 7,400,205 _____

C. 5,952,631 _____

D. 2,540,513 _____

E. 4,521,368 _____

F. 2,261,968 _____

G. 4,231,948 _____

Standard Form Notation

Write each number in **standard form**.

A. 500 + 90 + 6 _____

B. 2,000 + 400 + 60 + 7 _____

C. 40,000 + 3,000 + 800 + 20 + 1 _____

D. 200,000 + 50,000 + 7,000 + 10 + 4 _____

E. Write your own. _____

Dictionary Pronunciation

Listen to the vowel sounds in each word below. Draw a line
to connect each word with its **dictionary pronunciation**.

dream	(āt)
knot	(pĭk´ əl)
shirt	(rīt)
crew	(shûrt)
officer	(kŏm´ ət)
tense	(drēm)
write	(kro͞o)
mermaid	(mûr´ mād)
pickle	(nŏt)
eight	(ŏ´fə sûr)
comet	(tĕns)

Beginning Consonant Blends

Look at the **consonant blends** in the box below. Write a blend on each line to form a word that matches one of the pictures. Draw a line from the word to its picture.

cl	dr	sc	sk	sn	st

1. _____ake

2. _____oud

3. _____ess

4. _____ared

5. _____unk

6. _____ore

7. _____amp

8. _____um

9. _____irt

10. _____ock

Rounding Numbers

Round each number to the nearest **ten**.

A. 6,388 _____

B. 567,912 _____

C. 1,587,561 _____

D. 89,258 _____

Round each number to the nearest **hundred**.

E. 8,258 _____

F. 553 _____

G. 22,025 _____

H. 2,364 _____

Round each number to the nearest **thousand**.

I. 10,589 _____

J. 23,278 _____

K. 654,342 _____

L. 32,751 _____

Math

Understanding Place Value

Write the **place value** of the highlighted digit on the line.
The first one has been done for you.

A. 3,921 _____hundreds_____   B. 1,572 _____

C. 2,463 _____   D. 5,761 _____

E. 4,984 _____   F. 1,756 _____

G. 6,357 _____   H. 6,852 _____

Complete the Sentence

Reading Comprehension

Use the words from the word list to complete the sentences below.

Word List

insists	blend	borrow	dangerous
entire	proud	amazing	fond

1. The acrobats at the circus do _____ tricks.

2. Jan is _____ of her new classmate, Diana.

3. When you _____ blue and yellow, you get green.

4. Mom always _____ that I wear my seat belt.

5. Playing in the street can be _____.

6. I was _____ when I won first prize.

7. May I _____ your eraser?

8. Sarah drank the _____ carton of milk.

Ending Consonant Blends

Choose a **consonant blend** from the word list to complete a different word on each line.

1. ba_____
2. la_____
3. la_____
4. si_____
5. tru_____
6. ca_____
7. da_____
8. da_____
9. de_____

Word List

ft	sp
mp	nd
nk	nt
	st

10. ba_____
11. la_____
12. si_____
13. tru_____
14. tru_____
15. ca_____
16. da_____
17. de_____
18. cri_____

Understanding Place Value

Write the **place value** of the highlighted digit in the box.

A. 47,629

B. 35,116

C. 59,024

D. 23,199

E. 98,965

F. 78, 620

G. 83,456

H. 19,201

A Friendly Letter

Write a letter to your favorite actor or actress. Include all five parts of a friendly letter. Remember to put a comma after the greeting and closing.

_____

_____

_____

_____

_____

_____

_____

_____

_____

Addressing an Envelope

Address the envelope below using the information given.

The sender is:
Mr. Fred Barrow
216 Dawson Drive
Ogden, UT 66065

The receiver is:
Ms. Carla George
22 W. 42nd Street
Tampa, FL 21563

_____

_____

_____

_____

_____

_____

Identifying Types of Stories

Read each title below. Write **F** on the line if you believe the story is **fiction**,
NF if you think it is **nonfiction**, or **B** if you think it is a **biography**.

_____ **1.** Kelly's Rainbow Zebra

_____ **2.** Life in Jamestown

_____ **3.** How Cars Are Made

_____ **4.** We Rode on a Unicorn

_____ **5.** Plants of North America

_____ **6.** The Life of Albert Einstein

_____ **7.** My Trip to Mars

Fiction:	a story that is made-up or is not factual
Nonfiction:	a true or factual story
Biography:	a story about a real person's life

_____ **8.** Lincoln, the Sixteenth President

_____ **9.** Georgie, the Singing Monkey

_____ **10.** All about Susan B. Anthony

_____ **11.** The Battles of the Civil War

_____ **12.** The 10,000-Year-Old Woman

On the Road through Fourth Grade

Silent Letters

Draw a circle around the **silent letter** or **letters** in each word.

1. know	2. comb	3. kneel	4. light
5. ghastly	6. write	7. gnaw	8. wrap
9. gnat	10. knife	11. gnome	12. knock
13. knot	14. thumb	15. climb	16. tomb
17. wrench	18. knit	19. dough	20. knight
21. knee	22. gnu	23. wrist	24. gnarl

Two-Digit Addition

Circle the **even** answers. Draw a square around the **odd** answers.

A. 86 +45	B. 62 +95	C. 81 +55	D. 37 +87	E. 64 +56
F. 50 +58	G. 65 +70	H. 98 +14	I. 88 +58	J. 94 +21
K. 54 +87	L. 54 +64	M. 73 +15	N. 82 +41	O. 33 +45

Abbreviations

Write the correct abbreviation for each on the line beside it.
Use the abbreviations word list.

Apartment _____   Railroad _____   centimeter _____

Avenue _____   Road _____   Department _____

Boulevard _____   dozen _____   teaspoon _____

Building _____   Junior _____   hour _____

Word List

Bldg.	cm	tsp.	Apt.	Jr.	Ave.
Blvd.	Dept.	hr.	RR	dz.	Rd.

Classifying

Read the words in each box. Circle the word that **does not belong** with the others.

seven forty fork sixteen	July December Monday February
flour sugar milk kitchen	movie letter magazine book
owl kangaroo cantaloupe wolf	black house orange yellow

On the Road through Fourth Grade

Following Directions

Follow the directions to draw a picture in the box.

1. Draw a tree with four branches and orange and red leaves in the bottom left corner.
2. Draw a yellow half moon in the upper right corner.
3. Draw a brown fence across the bottom.
4. Draw four gray cats on the fence.
5. Draw six dark clouds in the sky.
6. Draw one owl on a branch of the tree.
7. Draw five black birds flying in the sky.
8. Add any other details you wish.

Break the Code

Find the sums. Write the letter next to each problem on the correct lines below to read the coded message.

```
    96          56          79          86          38          64
  + 58        + 86        + 38        + 27        + 87        + 83
   (I)         (V)         (D)         (E)         (K)         (D)
```

```
    89          58          73          86          69          77
  + 47        + 62        + 49        +76         + 52        + 54
   (U)         (G)         (A)         (Y)         (W)         (R)
```

___ ___ ___ ___   ___ ___ ___ ___   ___ ___ ___ ___
142 113 131 162   120 147 147 117   121 147 131 125

Categories of Words

Circle the three words that belong together in a category.

1.
golf   lawyer

artist   doctor

2.
train   car

airplane   glove

3.
lungs   brain

heart   food

4.
Canada   Texas

Virginia   Florida

5.
necklace   ring

balloon   bracelet

6.
happy   grumpy

embarrassed   laughter

Alphabetical Order

Write numbers in front of the words in each group to put them in **alphabetical order**.

A.	B.	C.
king	toast	egg
keen	toffee	elephant
kernel	told	ensemble
knee	tomorrow	elf
keep	total	electric
kind	together	ending
kangaroo	tough	especially

Using Math Symbols <, >, or =

Solve each problem. Print the answer next to the correct letter at the bottom.
Place the correct symbol (<, >, or =) in the circle.

A. 22 + 35 = _____   B. 60 + 39 = _____   C. 50 + 31 = _____

D. 63 + 20 = _____   E. 10 + 3 = _____   F. 50 + 25 = _____

G. 77 + 7 = _____   H. 60 + 21 = _____   I. 12 + 30 = _____

_____ ◯ _____ (A) (G)   _____ ◯ _____ (C) (H)

_____ ◯ _____ (B) (I)   _____ ◯ _____ (F) (E)

_____ ◯ _____ (D) (G)   _____ ◯ _____ (A) (G)

Cloze

Read the story below. Many words are missing.
Fill in the blanks with words from the word list.

Randy loved to paint. He liked to paint with his fingers _____
he was little. He would paint on _____. He would paint on
tables. Once he _____ painted on the living room wall!
Randy's _____ were not happy with his painting. They
_____ him to play ball or ride his _____,
but Randy only wanted to paint. When _____ was older, he
helped the neighbors paint _____ house. He painted
a huge but beautiful _____ on the front of their house. The
_____ did not want a huge, beautiful flower
_____ on the front of their house. Randy _____
that job! Today Randy is very happy. _____ is a famous
painter. Now his parents _____ his painting. And the
neighbors wish they still had the flower on the front of their house.

Word List

begged
bicycle
even
flower
He
lost
love
neighbors
painted
paper
parents
Randy
their
when

Three-Digit Addition

Add to solve each problem.

A. 486 + 514	B. 237 + 185	C. 902 + 404	D. 375 +612

E. 842 + 254	F. 951 + 726	G. 33 76 + 54	H. 45 48 + 85

Addition with Decimals

Add to solve each problem.

A.	3.5 + 8.2	B.	7.9 + 3.1	C.	9.0 + 4.8	D.	49.5 + 52.4
E.	7.03 + 7.85	F.	3.25 + 4.94	G.	8.03 + 5.13	H.	49.6 + 31.2

Syllables

Read the animal names below. Count the number
of **syllables** in each name. Print the number of syllables in the box.

rabbit		snake		elephant	
monkey		lion		giraffe	
flamingo		manatee		dinosaur	
koala		wolverine		dolphin	
whale		aardvark		emu	

Writing Paragraphs

Read the title and main idea of the paragraph. Write your own details.

Title of paragraph: My Best Friend

Main Idea: My best friend is someone special.

Details: 1. _____

2. _____

3. _____

4. _____

Retell the Main Idea: I am glad I have such a great friend.

Use the information above to write a paragraph. Include the main idea and details, then retell the main idea. Indent the first sentence. Use capital letters and periods. Remember to title the paragraph.

_____

_____

_____

_____

_____

_____

_____

_____

_____

Days of the Week Abbreviations

Write the **abbreviation** for each day of the week.
Then find each word in the word search below.

1. Sunday _____

2. Friday _____

3. Thursday _____

4. Saturday _____

5. Monday _____

6. Wednesday _____

7. Tuesday _____

```
M O N D A Y R G H W U
P T O L G F E A C E Y
D H S U N D A Y F D D
I U W J S D D P A N S
S R M T W T F S P E X
S S J F M A M F B S C
Y D J J S A O R P D V
G A N D O T F I P A B
F Y F T U E S D A Y H
H I O N E I S A O E J
S A T U R D A Y G L P
J M P Q W S L N T Y D
U E R L H T Y F Y J A
X I L W R V A O W P M
```

Context Clues

One word has been highlighted in each sentence below. There are two definitions given for the word. Decide which meaning is correct by reading the sentence and thinking about how the word is used. Circle the correct meaning.

1. The **bail** was broken, so the bucket of water was difficult to lift.
   a. throw water out   b. the handle of a pail

2. The princess had a grand time at the **ball** last night.
   a. a dance   b. a round object

3. Joe **left** before I could tell him good-bye.
   a. the opposite of right   b. went away

4. Jack had a **fit** when his brother broke his new bicycle.
   a. suitable   b. an attack

5. The group became **grave** when they saw the danger they were in.
   a. serious   b. a place of burial

Three-Digit Addition

Time yourself. How fast can you complete the problems?

A.
| 410 | 737 | 426 | 166 | 404 | 259 | 272 |
| + 291 | + 288 | + 497 | + 617 | + 395 | + 450 | + 438 |

B.
| 357 | 519 | 834 | 313 | 558 | 687 | 901 |
| + 417 | + 170 | + 196 | + 488 | + 184 | + 139 | + 149 |

Time: _____   Number correct: _____

Reading a Bar Graph

The bar graph below shows how many boxes of cookies were sold at Discovery Elementary School over an eight-week period. Use the graph to answer the questions.

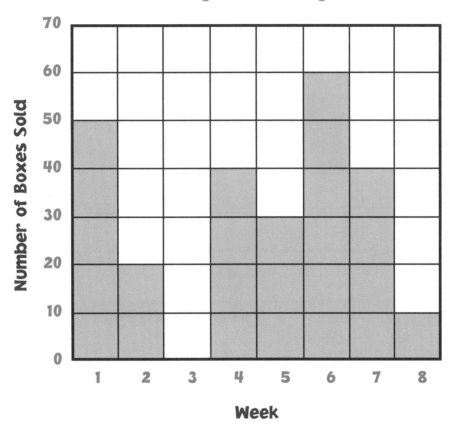

Boxes of Cookies Sold at Discovery Elementary School

A. What was the total number of boxes sold during the eight-week sale? _____

B. During which two weeks were the same number of boxes sold? _____

C. How many more boxes were sold during week 6 than week 7? _____

D. How many fewer boxes were sold during week 8 than week 2? _____

E. How many boxes were sold during week 3? _____ What do you think might

have happened? _____

Three-Digit Column Addition

Add to solve each problem.

A. 402 715 + 513	B. 800 240 + 912	C. 257 946 + 178	D. 589 456 + 981

E. 643 285 133 + 341	F. 321 419 444 + 750	G. 814 901 121 + 215	H. 136 912 978 + 222

Riddles

> Twenty white horses up a red hill.
> Now they chomp. Now they stomp.
> Now they stand still.
> What are they?

The words in the box make a riddle. They have a hidden meaning. Can you guess what the riddle is about? The answer is teeth! There are twenty white teeth in your mouth. The red hill is your gums. As you talk, they move up and down as if they are chomping and stomping. When you finish talking, they "stand still."

Riddles give a symbolic meaning to things. They have been used for thousands of years. In ancient times, wise people would often answer questions with riddles. It was believed that knowledge was precious, or of great value, and should not be given to everyone. If a person could solve a riddle, he was smart enough to know the answer.

1. What is the main idea of this story?
   a. Riddles are used as symbols.
   b. Riddles have been used for many years.
   c. Riddles are hard to figure out.

2. What is a riddle?_____
   _____
   _____

3. The word **precious** means:
   a. a lot of money
   b. meaning
   c. valuable

4. Instead of giving an answer, why did wise people speak in riddles?
   _____
   _____

Alphabetical Order

Write the months in **alphabetical order** on the lines.
Then, write the **abbreviation** beside each month. Circle the month of your birthday.

Word List

January	February	March	April	September	June
December	August	May	October	November	July

1. _____   7. _____

2. _____   8. _____

3. _____   9. _____

4. _____   10. _____

5. _____   11. _____

6. _____   12. _____

Word Problems

Solve each word problem.

A. Dexter made $5.00 washing cars on Monday, $2.75 on Tuesday, and $6.25 on Wednesday. How much money did Dexter make in the three days of car washing?

C. Kerry ate two oranges at breakfast and half an orange at lunch. At dinner, Kerry ate the other half of the orange from lunch. How many oranges did Kerry eat?

B. Missy took 114 pictures last June, 121 last July, and 109 last August. How many pictures did Missy take last summer?

D. Sandy sold 65 books at the book sale on Thursday, 231 books on Friday, and 111 more on Saturday. How many books did Sandy sell in three days?

Three-Digit Addition

Add to solve the problems.

A. 358
+ 227

B. 371
+ 389

C. 408
+ 159

D. 327
+ 196

E. 730
+197

F. 344
+ 523

G. 751
+ 225

H. 400
+127

I. 111
+ 345

J. 250
+178

K. 382
+ 160

L. 348
+ 436

M. 428
+ 150

N. 197
+ 402

O. 724
+ 150

P. 181
+ 199

Q. 451
+ 315

R. 613
+ 178

Cloze

Read the story below. Many words are missing.
Fill in the blanks with words from the word list.

Word List

danced
down
had
peeking
puddles
pulled
reached
red
stepped
Sure
was
weather
would

Hunting for a Rainbow

Maggie pulled the rubber boots on over her shoes. She slid into her yellow raincoat and _____ the front closed. This was just the _____ she had been hoping for. The sky _____ a light gray with bits of blue _____ through. Maggie knew that this time she _____ find what she was looking for. She _____ outside and opened the big, _____ umbrella over her head. The light rain _____ on the rounded top and quickly slid _____ the sides. Her boots splashed in the _____ as Maggie walked through them. The rain _____ almost stopped so Maggie hurried faster. She _____ the top of the hill and looked. _____ enough, this time she found it! Beyond the hill was a beautiful rainbow sparkling in the sun.

The Old Farmer and His Magic Bird

1

On his 80th birthday, something strange happened. As Arius was wandering in the forest looking for firewood, he fell over a fallen log. When he climbed back to his feet, the old man heard a wondrous sound unlike anything he'd ever heard. It was a song that sounded as if a hundred fairies were whistling to him.

He felt his way along the path toward the sound until he saw something on a branch in front of him. It was a tiny bird with wings of red and gold and a chest of blue and green. Arius had never seen anything so beautiful. Then he remembered the storyteller's tale. He knew the bird must be the rainbow warbler.

The bird did not stop singing until the farmer snuck up on it and covered it with his cloak. Happily, Arius made his way out of the forest and headed home.

3

A long time ago, there was an old farmer named Arius who was very tired of living a hard life. His back ached and his hands were crooked from years of digging and planting. He lived alone on a tiny farm far away from the nearest kingdom, and no one ever visited him.

Every morning, he would wake before dawn and tend to his crops. His garden gave him barely enough food to eat, and there was never anything left to sell. At night, he would sit in his small hut and feel his heart grow heavy and sad.

When Arius was a boy, a mysterious storyteller once told him of a magical bird called a rainbow warbler. If captured, the bird would make its owner young and rich forever. Now that Arius was old and alone, there wasn't a day that passed that he didn't wish he could find that bird. More than anything in the world, he wanted another chance at life.

2

As soon as he reached his hut, Arius placed the bird in a small wire cage. Then, tired after his adventure, he plopped down on his cot and fell asleep.

When he awoke the next morning, his back wasn't hurting like it normally did. His hands and fingers were no longer crooked and swollen with pain. Something had happened to him. He looked in the mirror and saw a face 50 years younger staring back at him. The old farmer was a young man again!

Arius was so excited, he ran out the front door and tripped. When he got up to see what he'd stumbled over, he saw a small wooden chest. Removing the lid, he found that it was filled with hundreds of gold coins. Not only was Arius a young man, but he was a rich one, too. The storyteller's tale had come true!

4

As the days passed, the farmer grew even younger and a new chest of gold appeared on his doorstep each morning. One day, Arius ventured into the kingdom and bought a huge new farm and all the things he ever wanted.

Wherever he went, he took the bird with him in its cage. He did not want to risk losing it. But as time went by, he started to notice that the beautiful creature seemed to be growing sadder. It never sang the beautiful song he'd heard in the forest. It never tried to fly or flutter its wings. Even its radiant colors were beginning to fade.

Arius also noticed that even though his body was getting younger and he had all the wealth he could want, his heart was still heavy and sad. Everything in his new garden dried up and stopped growing. Arius had youth but no one to share it with, because he avoided other people. He feared that they might try to steal the warbler from him if they learned its secret. So he sat alone every night in front of the fire with no one to talk to and nothing to do.

5

The days passed and soon Arius's youth faded away. Once again, he had the body of an 80-year-old man with a bent back and crooked hands. But somehow, it didn't matter to him. He felt better now that he knew the rainbow warbler was free. He moved back to his old farm and gave away all the things he'd bought with the chests of gold.

Then, one morning, as he was planting seeds in his garden, he heard a familiar noise. It was the sound of a hundred fairies whistling softly. He looked up in the sky, and there, circling above him, was the warbler with its beautiful colors restored. It had returned to him.

7

Then, one day, Arius discovered that the rainbow warbler had lost all of its color. It was now just a gray bird that did not sing. He was afraid that the bird might die. Somehow, that did not seem fair to Arius, and it made him sad to think about it. Why should such a beautiful creature be sacrificed just so he could look better in the mirror?

Arius took the cage outside, and, with a brief sigh, opened its door. Slowly, the bird hobbled out and flapped its wings. It looked at Arius for a moment and then flew off into the trees. The farmer watched it go and sadly waved good-bye.

6

Arius soon learned that there had been no need to keep the bird in a cage. It never left his side now that it was free, and although Arius did not have the body of a young man, his heart grew lighter and happier.

Every day, he awoke to the bird's gentle song. His garden blossomed and people came from miles around to buy the wonderful fruits and vegetables that he now grew. He was never lonely again, as he and the rainbow warbler lived together happily ever after.

8

Antonym Search

Match each pair of antonyms by connecting a word from the first column of the word list with a word from the second column. Then, find and circle each antonym pair in the word search. (Hint: Each pair of words is spelled across and down and shares one letter.) One pair has already been done for you.

Word List

left	little
big	right
small	late
early	close
open	large
fresh	go
stop	long
short	stale
hot	bottom
noisy	quiet
top	cold

Can You Spell?

Underline the **spelling error** in each sentence.
Write the **correct spelling** of the word on the line.

1. Are you goeing to the ball game?   _____

2. My room is very cleen.   _____

3. Ronnie baught some gum at the store.   _____

4. Tony payed $15.00 to get his bike fixed.   _____

5. Pepper makes Becky sneaze.   _____

6. Billy loves ice creem.   _____

7. Travis is very frendly.   _____

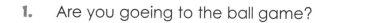

Math

Column Addition

Add to find the sums. Regroup if needed.

A.	33	B.	20	C.	23	D.	36
	45		37		14		25
	16		41		21		57
	21		19		26		19
	+ 25		+ 402		+ 382		+ 503

E.	456	F.	632	G.	254	H.	636
	219		169		513		258
	+ 387		+ 402		+ 382		+ 503

Alphabetical Order

Write the words from the word list in **alphabetical order** on the lines.

1. _____

2. _____

3. _____

4. _____

5. _____

6. _____

7. _____

8. _____

9. _____

10. _____

11. _____

12. _____

13. _____

14. _____

15. _____

16. _____

Word List

Mars	Venus
Mercury	Jupiter
Uranus	Neptune
satellite	universe
planet	shuttle
Earth	asteroid
Saturn	Pluto
moon	astronauts

Types of Sentences

Read each sentence. Using the key, write the corresponding letter on the line to name the sentence type. Then, write the correct **punctuation** at the end of the sentence.

_____ 1. Carol lives in a pretty house ☐

_____ 2. Does Joyce like peanut butter ☐

_____ 3. We miss Terry very much ☐

_____ 4. Take Timmy's cat to his house ☐

_____ 5. Wow, Kenneth hit a home run ☐

_____ 6. Ouch, that hurt ☐

Key

C = Command
E = Exclamation
S = Statement
Q = Question

Write an example of each of the following types of sentences.

Command _____

_____

Exclamation _____

_____

Question _____

_____

Statement _____

_____

Compound Words

Write a word from the word list on each line to form a **compound word**.
Find each compound word in the word search at the bottom of the page.

Word List

work	brush	noon	foot	ball	board
burger	stick	fall	corn	mark	bell

after _____

bare _____

book _____

cheese _____

water _____

pop _____

tooth_____

skate _____

candle_____

base_____

home_____

door _____

```
F B B C S J H O M E W O R K K
M A O D H K J J L X W J J C X
J S O O H E D N K K U F I I M
X E K O P E E C C X S T Y R D
B B M R Y B M S R G S I L F P
A A A B Y S C L E E F Z T U O
R L R E Y M R N L B Y F A E P
E L K L J B J D W I U O K E C
F A D L M S N H Z I V R J T O
O A C P R A B E I W A B G Q R
O P T R C S C F A L M M H E N
T R F D M W A T E R F A L L R
S K A T E B O A R D M S O C C
X U Z M M T O O T H B R U S H
A F T E R N O O N J H T V P S
```

Building Vocabulary

Beth wants to be a paramedic and she practices on her dog, Gumbo. Read the story to see how Gumbo feels about all of this. Then, read each of the five sentences. Write the letter for the best answer on the line.

Good Old Gumbo . . .

No dog was ever as patient as Gumbo. Just ask Beth. She is his owner. Beth has put Gumbo through a great deal in his young life. He's been a model for **assorted** doll clothes. He's **retrieved** baseballs from under thick hedges. Now Gumbo is a model again. This time it's for splints and bandages.

Beth is learning all about first aid. She hopes to be a paramedic one day. She thinks helping people would be a good thing. She wants to practice every bandage and splint on Gumbo.

After only five minutes, Gumbo has become **disturbed.** He doesn't think being wrapped up is much fun. He decides that he'd better do something **immediately.** He has heard the saying, "being all tied up." Gumbo wants to get out of this while he still can!

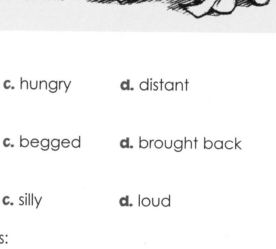

_____ 1. The word **assorted** means:
   a. tired   **b.** mixed   **c.** hungry   **d.** distant

_____ 2. The word **retrieved** means:
   a. bought   **b.** made   **c.** begged   **d.** brought back

_____ 3. The word **disturbed** means:
   a. upset   **b.** soft   **c.** silly   **d.** loud

_____ 4. The word **immediately** means:
   a. now   **b.** inside   **c.** under   **d.** never

_____ 5. A word in the story that is a synonym of **bound** is:
   a. owner   **b.** learning   **c.** tied   **d.** wrapped

Practice New Words

On a separate sheet of paper, write one sentence using each of these words:

assorted   retrieved   disturbed   immediately

Main Idea

The **main idea** of a paragraph is its central thought or topic. Read each paragraph. Read the three phrases under each paragraph. Decide which one tells the main idea. Write the letter of that phrase on the line.

_____ 1.   Gary and Fritz have been writing to each other for four years. Gary lives in Indiana and Fritz lives in Germany. Gary looks forward to Fritz's letters. Fritz usually sends at least one picture and sometimes he sends extra German stamps for Gary's collection. Gary and Fritz both hope that they can meet someday. They feel as if they know each other already.

      a. Pictures from Germany   **b.** Gary's German pen pal   **c.** Gary's friend

_____ 2.   Mary has been blind all of her life. She has gone to special schools to learn to do things for herself. Her best friend Katy is not blind. Katy and Mary help each other. Mary is trying to teach Katy to read Braille. It is a special system of raised dots that lets Mary "read" the page. Katy isn't doing very well at all. Katy says that it is hard for her to "see" the letters with her fingers.

      a. Learning to read   **b.** Understanding Braille   **c.** A special friendship

What's Missing?

Print the correct number in the box to complete each number sentence.

A. $2 + \boxed{} = 13$ **B.** $38 - \boxed{} = 24$ **C.** $28 - \boxed{} = 15$

D. $73 + \boxed{} = 89$ **E.** $40 - \boxed{} = 33$ **F.** $82 + \boxed{} = 97$

G. $55 + \boxed{} = 73$ **H.** $56 - \boxed{} = 13$ **I.** $19 + \boxed{} = 33$

J. $26 + \boxed{} = 35$ **K.** $28 - \boxed{} = 19$ **L.** $77 - \boxed{} = 59$

Two-Digit Subtraction Review

Calculate the following **subtraction** problems. Regroup as needed.

A. 15
  − 5

B. 25
  − 3

C. 10
  − 2

D. 19
  − 5

E. 14
  − 5

F. 16
  − 4

G. 19
  − 2

H. 21
  − 7

I. 40
  − 5

J. 62
  − 9

K. 28
  − 16

L. 38
  − 12

M. 42
  − 7

N. 46
  − 25

O. 28
  − 14

Analogies

Fill in the blanks to complete the **analogies**.

1. A **mouth** is to **taste** as an **eye** is to _____.

2. A **person** is to a **house** as a **bear** is to a _____.

3. An **apple** is to a **tree** as a **watermelon** is to a _____.

4. A **kitten** is to a **cat** as a **puppy** is to a _____.

5. An **inch** is to **length** as a **pound** is to _____.

6. A **car** is to a **road** as a **boat** is to _____.

7. A **whale** is to **water** as an **elephant** is to _____.

Nouns and Verbs

Read each sentence below. Underline each **noun**. Circle each **verb**.

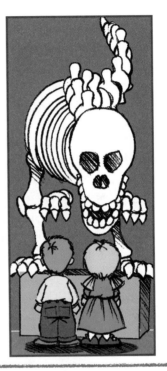

1. Ryan and Cathy went to the museum.

2. Beverly washes the big, green car.

3. The big, black dog scared Chris.

4. Wanda lives in Georgia.

5. Don owns a large store.

6. The warm night was peaceful.

7. The girl was late for practice.

8. Brian put the blue sweater in the dryer.

9. Amber had fun at the park.

Regroup or Not to Regroup?

Subtract to find each difference.

A. 63 − 21	B. 45 − 25	C. 75 − 23	D. 33 − 11	E. 46 − 21

F. 32 − 15	G. 55 − 27	H. 90 − 42	I. 75 − 68	J. 35 − 16

Building Vocabulary

Davey has a new friend who keeps bothering him. Read the story to find out more. Then, read each of the five sentences. Write the letter for the best answer on the line.

A Fishing Friend

It all began last summer when Davey was fishing at his grandpa's farm. Suddenly, something odd **occurred**. A big head **emerged** from the water. Davey was **terrified** at first. The creature smiled and told Davey that his name was Clarence.

Clarence told Davey that he had always been alone and was tired of his **solitude**. He wanted a friend. Davey felt sorry for Clarence and tried his best to cheer him up.

Now it seems that Davey has a friend for life. There's just one problem: Clarence wants to be with Davey all the time. Davey can't go fishing alone anymore. He hopes Clarence will find another new friend soon. Davey would like some of his own solitude. He would also like to catch some fish. Few fish come around when Clarence is near!

_____ 1. The word **occurred** means:
 a. pointed   **b.** painted   **c.** scraped   **d.** happened

_____ 2. The word **emerged** means:
 a. fell in   **b.** came out   **c.** divided   **d.** twisted around

_____ 3. The word **terrified** means:
 a. scared   **b.** rich   **c.** healthy   **d.** ripped

_____ 4. The word **solitude** means:
 a. teacher   **b.** friends   **c.** leaving   **d.** being alone

_____ 5. A word in the story that is a synonym for **desired** is:
 a. wanted   **b.** problem   **c.** cheer   **d.** destroyed

Practice New Words

On a separate sheet of paper, write one sentence using each of these words:

occurred   emerged   terrified   solitude

Beat the Clock (Double-Digit Subtraction)

Make several copies of this page. Time yourself every day for a week.
Does your time improve? Does your accuracy increase?

A.

86	90	42	94	62	55	41
− 58	− 29	− 28	− 66	− 49	− 17	− 25

B.

75	47	40	61	54	81	67
− 17	− 18	− 29	− 23	− 38	− 27	− 38

C.

91	52	43	71	75	84	61
− 56	− 49	− 38	− 34	− 46	− 47	− 12

D.

93	84	82	84	66	75	54
− 75	− 19	− 73	− 37	− 48	− 27	− 39

E.

87	74	67	71	83	41	71
− 38	− 25	− 38	− 64	− 28	− 34	− 42

Time: _____   **Number correct:** _____

More Nouns and Verbs

Look at the words in the word list.
Write the **nouns** on the building.
Write the **verbs** on the rocket.

Word List

pretend
news
remove
school
cow
be
earth
flee
sell
lamp
car
took
speak
hear
berry
lake
bring
heart
window
understand
easel
wear

Plurals (-s or -es)

Add the correct ending (**s** or **es**) to make each word **plural**.
Write the new words on the lines.

1. teacher _____

2. potato _____

3. house _____

4. kite _____   10. friend _____

5. class _____   11. clock _____

6. clown _____   12. computer _____

7. box _____   13. couch _____

8. handbook _____   14. carmel _____

9. watch _____   15. fox _____

Adding & Subtracting with Decimals   Math

Add or subtract to solve each problem.

A.	7.0 + 7.5	B.	9.2 – 4.1	C.	8.3 + 2.8
D.	23.5 – 16.3	E.	4.23 + 1.95	F.	6.35 – 4.96
G.	2.98 + 6.85	H.	96.3 – 21.4	I.	6.91 + 2.98

Story Problems

Solve each word problem.

A. Shannon bought 3 dozen eggs at the store. On the way home, she dropped the egg cartons and 13 of the eggs broke. How many unbroken eggs does Shannon now have? _____

B. Dawn is allowed to swim in the pool for 60 minutes each day. If she has been swimming today for 25 minutes, how many more minutes does she have left in the pool? _____

C. There were 937 students at Ridge Hill School. If 43 students missed school due to illness, how many students were at school? _____

D. Phil's Used Car Lot had 142 cars to sell. If Phil sold 26 of the cars, how many did he have left to sell? _____

E. Together, Cindy and Jim counted 221 cars on their road trip. Cindy counted 132 of the cars. How many cars did Jim count? _____

Categories

Read each group of words or phrases. Choose the best category name from the box. Write the correct category under each list. The first one has been done for you.

Categories:

types of berries	summer clothing
things during a storm	baby animals
~~yellow things~~	

1.
A. sun
B. banana
C. daisy
D. corn
E. lemon

2.
A. bathing suit
B. sunglasses
C. shorts
D. sandals
E. short-sleeved shirt

3.
A. strawberry
B. raspberry
C. blackberry
D. blueberry
E. boysenberry

4.
A. foal
B. lamb
C. chick
D. duckling
E. kitten

Category: | Category: | Category: | Category:

yellow things | _____ | _____ | _____

Possessive Plurals

Make each highlighted word **possessive** by rewriting the word on the line
and adding an apostrophe in the correct place.

1. That is **Danas** dollhouse. _____

2. **Craigs** truck is very big. _____

3. I like **Sharons** new green bicycle. _____

4. The **childrens** song was perfectly in tune. _____

5. The two **girls** kites flew high in the sky. _____

6. The **schools** end-of-the-year picnic was fun. _____

7. The **trucks** loud horn scared Barbara. _____

8. The **actors** costume was colorful. _____

9. I love to visit my **grandmothers** house. _____

10. The **singers** voices are beautiful. _____

11. Those **dogs** collars are green. _____

Three- and Four-Digit Subtraction

Subtract to solve each problem. Circle the smallest answer.
Draw a square around the largest answer.

A.   912
  − 735

B.   583
  − 321

C.   185
  − 112

D.   635
  − 504

E.   865
  − 125

F.   999
  − 428

G. 2,190
 − 1,065

H. 5,948
 − 2,374

Three-Digit Subtraction

Subtract to solve each problem. Circle all the even numbers.

A.
423	222	435	628	757	637	423
− 285	− 153	− 166	− 499	− 178	−388	− 285

B.
326	972	685	518	741	438	371
− 285	− 609	− 246	− 329	− 362	− 258	− 283

C.
529	625	514	664	742	200	634
− 482	− 407	− 126	− 278	− 467	− 158	− 277

Adjectives

Underline the **adjectives** in each paragraph below.
The first adjective has been underlined for you.

1. I like <u>chocolate</u> ice cream. Chocolate ice cream tastes good when it is hot outside. Unfortunately, chocolate ice cream makes a big, sticky mess. I solve this problem by eating my yummy, chocolate ice cream outside.

2. One sunny day, I found a white rabbit hopping in front of my house. I walked up to the frightened rabbit and talked to him. He finally calmed down and I picked him up. His soft fur tickled my hands. I took the sweet rabbit behind my house to the big forest. Waiting there for him was his happy mother. the two small rabbits hopped home together.

Persuasive Paragraph

You must convince your mom to let you go bowling.
Ask her, give your reasons, and then ask again.

Title of paragraph: _____

Question: May I _____

Reasons: 1. _____

2. _____

3. _____

4. _____

Ask again: _____

Use the information above to write a paragraph. Ask the question.
State the reasons, and then ask the question again. Indent the first
sentence. Use capital letters and periods. Remember to give your
paragraph a title.

_____

_____

_____

_____

_____

_____

_____

_____

_____

Abbreviations

Write the correct **abbreviation** for each word on the line next to it.
Use a dictionary to check your answers for spelling and capitalization.

Street _____   pound _____   minute _____

Junior _____   ounce _____   foot _____

Mister _____   Senior _____   inch _____

Doctor _____   centimeter _____   President _____

Apartment _____   Road _____   Mountain _____

Subtraction Review

Subtract to solve each problem.

A.
```
  623      900      722      377      871      628
- 194    - 309    - 317    - 186    - 384    - 300
```

B.
```
  990      818      572      951      825      771
- 731    - 693    - 335    - 357    - 469    - 217
```

Write the answers in order from smallest to largest.

_____   _____   _____   _____   _____

_____   _____   _____   _____   _____

Subtraction with Decimals

Subtract to solve each problem.

A.	20.20 − 13.75	**B.**	334.5 − 145.6	**C.**	7.051 − 2.058
D.	3.812 − 2.116	**E.**	8.229 − 2.443	**F.**	421.6 − 334.7

Contractions

Read each sentence. Circle the correct **contraction** for the highlighted words.

1.	I **did not** look at the movie when it was scary!	didn't	did'nt	don't
2.	**You are** my best friend!	You'd	You'll	You're
3.	Are you sure **we are** on the right path?	we'd	we'll	we're
4.	Brian said **he is** older than you.	he'd	he's	he'll
5.	**Who would** want to live in that dusty old house?	Who'd	Who's	Who've
6.	**They are** very kind people.	They'll	They're	They've
7.	**Let us** begin the lesson.	Lets	Let's	Lets'
8.	**You are** going to be late for school.	Your'e	You're	Your
9.	**You have** given me plenty of reasons to study.	You'd	You're	You've
10.	**I am** going to the zoo tomorrow.	I'd	I'll	I'm

Pronouns

Read each sentence. Replace the highlighted word(s)
with the correct pronoun by writing it on the lines.

1. **Jim and Carla** like to ride motorcycles. _____ ride whenever they can.

2. **Jane** has two lovebirds. _____ sings to them every day.

3. **Chelsea and Cheyna** are sisters. Let's go to their house and play with _____.

4. **Billy** is a police officer. _____ likes to help people.

5. **This book** is from my grandparents. _____ is my favorite.

6. **Daphne and I** like jelly beans. _____ like to eat the red ones.

7. That is **Rocky**'s baseball. Please give it to _____.

Subtraction with Decimals

A.	8.5 − 2.8	**B.**	9.2 − 7.5	**C.**	7.1 − 4.1		
D.	3.75 − 2.12	**E.**	54.3 − 19.4	**F.**	9.35 − 5.68		
G.	2.01 − 1.95	**H.**	5.12 − 4.08	**I.**	53.0 − 22.6		

If the answers were dollar amounts, which problem would you like? ☐

Building Vocabulary

Ike and Spike are two young boys. Read the story to find out some of the messes they get themselves involved in. Then, read each of the five sentences. Write the letter for the best answer on the line.

Ike, Spike, and the Circle Game

Ike and Spike are two brave little boys who will try anything once. There's just one problem. These nine-year-old friends can never agree. They always want to do things in different ways. That's quite a **dilemma** sometimes!

Once they **created** a large mural. Ike's faces were smiling, and Spike's faces all frowned. Another day, the boys went for a long hike. Ike took the path up into the hills, and Spike walked down by the river. They didn't find each other again until the next day.

Here you see them **struggling** to get home from a fishing **excursion**. Each boy wants to go a different way. These poor guys have been spinning in circles for an hour. Maybe soon one will get tired so they can at least move the boat!

_____ 1. The word **dilemma** means:
   a. canoe   **b.** problem   **c.** bait   **d.** song

_____ 2. The word **created** means:
   a. made   **b.** heard   **c.** told   **d.** found

_____ 3. The word **struggling** means:
   a. laughing   **b.** running   **c.** trying hard   **d.** painting

_____ 4. The word **excursion** means:
   a. hat   **b.** lesson   **c.** trip   **d.** fort

_____ 5. A word in the story that is a synonym for **varied** is:
   a. ordinary   **b.** poor   **c.** problem   **d.** different

Practice New Words

On a separate sheet of paper, write one sentence using each of these words:

dilemma   **created**   **struggling**   **excursion**

Mixed Problems with Decimals

Add or **subtract** to solve each problem.

List the answers
from largest to smallest.

A. 726.6
      + 122.5

B. 9.025
      − 1.874

C. 423.8
      + 111.4

D. 8.345
      + 2.137

E. 77.61
      − 44.32

F. 522.7
      + 311.7

_____

_____

_____

_____

_____

_____

Using Guide Words

Look at the words in the word list. Print each word in alphabetical order
below the two **guide words** it would appear between in a dictionary.

1. aardvark   afghan

_____

_____

_____

_____

2. Africa   aim

_____

_____

_____

_____

Word List

aggravate
above
aboard
affect
about
after
aid
agree
ailment
afford

Understanding What I've Read

Parasites

Some animals get their food by living in or on other things. These animals, called parasites, do not kill the animals they live on, but they may harm or irritate them. A flea will live on a dog, cat, or other animals. The animal it lives on is called the host. The flea gets its food by sucking the other animal's blood. The flea will not harm the host, but it will make the host itch and feel uncomfortable. Some worms are also parasites. A tapeworm lives inside the body of an animal. It eats the food the host has eaten. The tapeworm can make the host very sick. Plants can be parasites, too. Mistletoe and some types of ferns live on trees, taking food and water from them.

1. What is the main idea of this story?
   a. Parasites live on or in other living things.
   b. A flea is a parasite.
   c. Parasites can make their hosts sick.

2. How does a flea get food?

   _____

3. Where does a tapeworm live?

   _____

4. What is a parasite? _____

   _____

5. What does the word **host** mean?
   a. an animal that lives on another living thing
   b. the animal a parasite lives on
   c. mistletoe

6. What kinds of plants can be parasites?

   _____

Beat the Clock (Multiplication Facts 0 to 9)

A.

7	4	3	9	1	8	2	6	0	5
x 4	x 6	x 1	x 5	x 4	x 4	x 3	x 8	x 6	x 5

B.

8	4	0	4	3	6	7	1	8	2
x 1	x 0	x 3	x 3	x 5	x 3	x 3	x 0	x 9	x 7

C.

5	2	8	0	5	4	1	9	3	6
x 4	x 0	x 7	x 0	x 1	x 7	x 6	x 1	x 8	x 0

D.

7	4	2	6	9	0	5	7	1	3
x 1	x 9	x 4	x 7	x 0	x 7	x 9	x 6	x 3	x 4

E.

0	8	3	5	1	9	5	2	6	4
x 9	x 5	x 2	x 6	x 1	x 4	x 0	x 2	x 2	x 5

F.

7	3	1	8	6	4	2	8	0	5
x 7	x 9	x 5	x 0	x 6	x 1	x 6	x 3	x 2	x 2

G.

9	1	7	4	0	5	9	2	8	3
x 3	x 9	x 0	x 4	x 5	x 8	x 9	x 1	x 8	x 0

H.

2	6	6	1	7	4	0	9	3	7
x 8	x 1	x 9	x 7	x 5	x 8	x 1	x 8	x 7	x 9

I.

5	0	6	3	5	2	8	7	1	9
x 7	x 8	x 4	x 3	x 3	x 9	x 6	x 2	x 2	x 7

J.

8	3	0	7	2	9	1	9	4	6
x 2	x 6	x 4	x 8	x 5	x 2	x 8	x 6	x 2	x 5

Time: _____   **Number correct:** _____

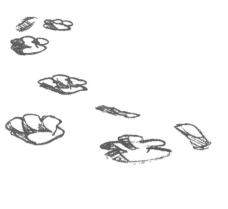

The Monster's Footprints

1

He led her across the street to the field by Oscar Sampson's farm. Tim's older sister, Alice, was standing by the fence, staring out into space.

"Hi, Alice," Kelly said. "What are you looking at?"

Alice pointed at the field. "Do you see them?" she asked.

Kelly shook her head, but then she noticed three sets of tracks in the snow heading across the field toward the barn. The tracks in the center were much larger than the other two.

Kelly shrugged. "So? What's so unusual about tracks in the snow?"

"Look closer," Tim replied.

3

It seemed like Kelly Hoover's lucky day. An unexpected snowstorm the night before had closed school for the day. She wolfed down her breakfast, put on her coat and boots, and was outside before the clock struck eight.

Her little neighbor Tim was already waiting for her in the front yard. He was a pest, but Tim's father was a refrigerator salesman, and the cardboard boxes he brought home were fun to build forts with—especially snow forts. So Kelly was happy to see him.

But Tim had something else in mind. "You've got to see this!" he exclaimed as soon as she stepped out the door. "Follow me!"

2

Kelly climbed over the fence and examined the tracks. She noticed that the two small ones were boot prints.

"Those were ours," Alice pointed out.

The tracks in the center looked like giant bare footprints with toes as big as soda cans.

"They go all the way up to Mr. Sampson's barn," said Tim. "Then, they stop and reappear on the other side, like whatever it was just walked through solid walls."

"Then where do they go?" Kelly asked.

"To Mr. Sampson's house, and then they stop. Do you think he's a monster? Or a ghost? Maybe, the Abdominal Snowman or something?"

Kelly frowned. "You mean Abominable. And no, I don't think Mr. Sampson's a monster. That's goofy."

"But he's so mean!" Alice exclaimed. "Once he yelled at us for petting his dog."

"That's because Sniffer's dangerous. He bites," Kelly replied.

"Still, he didn't have to yell."

4

"Let's get to the bottom of this," said Kelly. "There's no such thing as monsters, but something had to make these footprints. Let's find out what."

The three kids made their way across the field, being careful not to step on the strange tracks. They followed them all the way to the barn where they stopped just as Tim had said. They walked around the barn, and sure enough, the footprints reappeared as if whatever it was had just walked through the barn's walls.

"Told you it was a monster," said Alice with her hands on her hips.

5

The three of them tiptoed to the other side of the barn. Kelly knelt down beside one of the tracks and nearly stuck her whole face in the snow as she examined the track.

A minute later, she stood up and held a tiny piece of brown paper between her finger and thumb. "I've solved the mystery," she said.

"How?" Tim and Alice asked at the same time.

Kelly put her arms behind her back and walked around the two of them as she explained her solution. "At first," she said, "I thought this was just a simple prank, but then I realized it was an act of revenge."

"Revenge?" Tim and Alice asked again.

"Yes. My first idea was that someone was trying to scare people. But how could they make the tracks without making tracks of their own? Perhaps they had a hot-air balloon and a very long pole with fake feet attached. That way they could make the prints and fly over the barn so it would look like the monster walked through the barn."

7

Suddenly, there came a loud shout from the farmhouse. Oscar Sampson waved at them from the porch. "What are you kids doing over there? Why are you on my property?" he roared.

Tim and Alice tried to run away, but Kelly caught both of them by their collars. "We're sorry, Mr. Sampson," she shouted back. "It's just that we found these very strange tracks, and we were wondering what they were."

"You kids go home before I call your parents!" the old farmer replied. He went back inside and slammed the door.

"See?" Alice cried. "He doesn't want us to look because we'll figure out that he's a monster!"

"For the last time, Mr. Sampson is not a monster!" Kelly exclaimed. "But let's go to the other side of the barn, so he can't see us. I want to take a closer look at one of these footprints."

6

"Howie Stevens has a hot air balloon," said Alice.

"Yes, but he also has a snowplow. If you remember, he was plowing our driveways this morning, not riding around in his balloon." Then, Kelly smiled. "So I looked closer at a footprint and found this." She showed them the piece of brown paper again.

"What's that?" asked Tim.

"I think you know what it is—both of you. It's from a piece of cardboard. Someone cut out big cardboard footprints and attached a couple of broomsticks or something to them. Then they made these tracks by pressing the footprints into the snow. Of course, the problem is, their own boot prints had to be right beside them." Kelly rubbed her chin. "Now let's see. Who has a lot of cardboard?"

Tim and Alice stared at the snow. "I know Mr. Sampson yelled at you," Kelly continued, "but that's no reason for trying to make people think he's a monster."

"We're very sorry," Tim said sadly.

"Yeah," Alice added. "It wasn't a nice thing to do."

Kelly sighed. "Maybe you should tell that to Mr. Sampson."

8

Prefixes

Use the prefix bank and word list to **create as many words as you can**.
Write the words on the lines. Use another sheet of paper if needed.

Prefix Bank

dis- in- pre- re- un-

Word List

able	dent
form	charge
close	qualify
fill	related
civilized	sole
miss	pay
capable	heat
come	cover
wind	view

1. _____
2. _____
3. _____
4. _____
5. _____
6. _____
7. _____
8. _____
9. _____
10. _____
11. _____
12. _____
13. _____
14. _____
15. _____
16. _____
17. _____
18. _____
19. _____
20. _____
20. _____
22. _____

How Many?

Multiply. Circle all the **odd** answers.

A.
11	7	10	12	5	9	12
x 6	x 8	x 6	x 6	x 9	x 4	x 5

B.
10	9	11	3	8	10	7
x 4	x 3	x 7	x 8	x 8	x 2	x 9

C.
11	10	2	8	10	11	10
x 2	x 9	x 9	x 5	x 1	x 9	x 7

Building Vocabulary

Gordy the gorilla and Tussie the elephant are good friends. Read the story to learn more about one of their adventures. Then, read each of the five sentences. Write the letter for the best answer on the line.

Friends to the End

Tussie and Gordy are the best of friends. After all, they are the two largest and loudest creatures in the jungle. There was a time when they feared each other. Now they find that they can **actually** help each other. Sometimes Gordy will scrub Tussie's huge, gray back. Tussie returns the **favor** by making her trunk into a shower for Gordy.

Once they **combined** efforts to do something quite **noble**. A newborn tiger cub had wandered into the jungle. The cub's parents were worried and came to Gordy and Tussie for help. Tussie made big, wide paths through the thick jungle. Gordy swung from tree to tree looking everywhere. Together, in an hour's time, they found the tiger cub. Everyone was pleased!

_____ 1. The word **actually** means:
    a. slowly   **b.** hotly   **c.** angrily   **d.** really

_____ 2. The word **favor** means:
    a. drink   **b.** good deed   **c.** surprise   **d.** dark night

_____ 3. The word **combined** means:
    a. pointed   **b.** slid   **c.** joined   **d.** yelled

_____ 4. The word **noble** means:
    a. furry   **b.** good   **c.** calm   **d.** bad

_____ 5. A word in the story that is a synonym for **searching** is:
    a. scrubbing   **b.** worried   **c.** looking   **d.** pleasing

Practice New Words

On a separate sheet of paper, write one sentence using each of these words:

    actually   favor   combined   noble

Find the Missing Factors

Write the missing **factor** to complete each fact.

A. 4 x □ = 12   □ x 5 = 0   8 x □ = 40

B. □ x 3 = 24   3 x □ = 27   □ x 9 = 63

C. 5 x □ = 35   □ x 1 = 18   9 x □ = 18

D. 6 x □ = 36   □ x 6 = 30   □ x 9 = 45

Homonyms

Read each sentence below.
Circle the **homonym** that completes each sentence correctly.

1. While in the woods, Kristen saw a (**bear   bare**).

2. Candy fell and hurt her (**tow   toe**).

3. The (**sale   sail**) on the boat billowed in the wind.

4. Sherry did not feel well and looked (**pail   pale**).

5. Teddy does not (**know   no**) how to play basketball.

6. We went to the mailbox and (**cent   sent**) a letter.

7. My cat had six kittens and four of them are (**mail   male**).

8. Sissy stopped to pick a (**flour   flower**) from the garden.

Multiplication Word Problems

Use **multiplication** to solve each word problem.

A. Stephen, Wendy, and Spencer each spent $9 at the amusement park. How much money did they spend altogether? $_____

B. Jennifer likes to make dolls. If she makes 3 dolls each day for 6 days, how many dolls will she have made? _____ **dolls**

C. Tory keeps his race cars in shoe boxes. He has 11 boxes with 5 cars in each. How many race cars does Tory have? _____ **race cars**

D. Tamika rode her bike for 2 hours every day for 8 days. How many hours did she ride altogether in those 8 days? _____ **hours**

E. Justin, Dylan, and Stephanie all wear hats. If they each have 12 hats, how many hats do they have altogether? _____ **hats**

F. Ursula had 3 mother cats. Each mother cat had 5 kittens. How many kittens did Ursula's cats have altogether? _____ **kittens**

G. Sean collects postage stamps. He puts 12 stamps on each page of his album. If Sean has 8 filled pages, how many stamps does Sean have? _____ **stamps**

H. Denise built 7 towers with building blocks. If she used 8 blocks for each tower, how many blocks did she use in all? _____ **blocks**

I. Gina wants to make friendship necklaces. She will use 9 beads on each necklace. How many beads does Gina need to make 5 necklaces? _____ **beads**

Compare and Contrast

Fill in the blanks to compare and contrast a newspaper and a book.
The first one has been done for you.

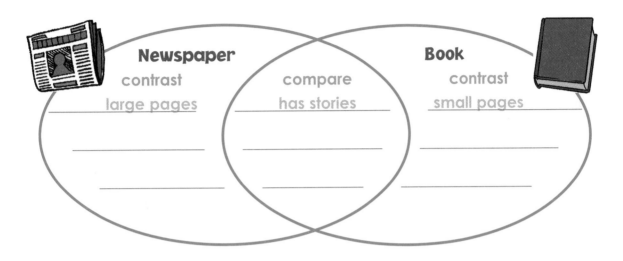

Newspaper
contrast
large pages

Book
contrast
small pages

compare
has stories

Write two paragraphs below. In the first paragraph, tell how newspapers
and books are alike. Tell how each is different in the second paragraph.
Be sure to indent the first sentence of each paragraph.

_____

_____

_____

_____

_____

_____

_____

_____

_____

_____

_____

Match the Fact to the Answer

4 x 5 =	8	1 x 5 =	24	6 x 3 =	40
2 x 7 =	18	5 x 3 =	5	0 x 9 =	6
8 x 1 =	20	3 x 8 =	12	1 x 7 =	0
9 x 2 =	15	2 x 6 =	21	8 x 5 =	18
5 x 3 =	14	7 x 3 =	15	6 x 1 =	7

Proper Nouns

Underline each **proper noun** in the story below. Write the correct capital letter above each proper noun. The first one has been done for you.

         C

Last <u>christmas</u> mom, dad, billy, isabel, and I went to aunt mable and uncle

buddy's house. All of our relatives were there having a good time. keisha, taylor,

and maya all got new sneakers from santa claus. alex and kelli brought a pie for

mrs. davis. The twins, dustin and dillon, showed off their new baby sister, stephanie.

jamie brought her new doll. Everyone had a good time and looks forward to getting

together on new year's day.

Understanding What I've Read

Space Probes

We learn about planets by observing, or studying, them. Scientists use telescopes to see planets. A telescope is a special instrument that makes faraway objects look bigger. Some planets are too far away to see clearly, even when we use a telescope. How can we learn about these planets? Scientists send special spacecraft called probes into space. Telescopes and cameras are sent in the probe to record everything they see. Probes also carry special instruments to examine the weather and soil on other planets. The information is sent back to Earth where scientists can study it. The first probe, called *Mariner 2*, was launched in 1962. It gave us information about the planet Venus. Since then, scientists have sent over 25 probes into space. Each probe tells us even more about other planets.

1. What is the main idea of this story?
   a. Probes tell us about other planets.
   b. Telescopes help us to see other planets.
   c. *Mariner 2* was the first space probe.

2. What is a probe?

   _____

3. What information about other planets can a probe gather?

   _____

4. What does the word **observe** mean?
   a. a special instrument
   b. to study
   c. probe

5. What special equipment do probes carry?

   _____

A Multiplication Puzzle

9	4	7	5	16	6	28	7	1	9	4	36	5	18
1	6	0	4	5	7	35	6	56	4	8	5	7	3
2	18	4	3	8	7	0	5	35	2	21	0	3	36
45	2	45	2	40	3	42	2	9	5	4	4	21	14
0	8	36	7	27	0	10	1	6	7	5	9	3	5
35	16	9	12	3	9	27	2	54	4	20	8	5	1
8	5	27	3	(3 x 6 = 18)		4	7	4	42	3	3	9
7	7	2	15	0	54	12	7	0	0	14	2	2	9
0	6	6	36	9	1	30	3	8	72	7	10	70	24
8	42	7	64	8	4	54	1	2	8	7	56	21	2
5	36	18	8	9	9	48	6	0	9	3	4	40	3

Solve the problems on the list. Find each problem in the puzzle and fill in the **x** and **=**. Circle the problems. One has been done for you.

Problem List

3 x 6 = ___18___   4 x 5 = _____

8 x 7 = _____   9 x 6 = _____

3 x 3 = _____   6 x 6 = _____

5 x 7 = _____   7 x 3 = _____

2 x 8 = _____   7 x 10 = _____

1 x 9 = _____   9 x 4 = _____

7 x 6 = _____   5 x 8 = _____

Descriptive Writing

The three adjectives below describe the picture. Add two more adjectives of your own. Write a paragraph about the picture using these adjectives. Remember to indent the first sentence of your paragraph and to include a title.

1. cheesy   2. messy   3. spicy

4. _____   5. _____

_____

_____

_____

_____

_____

Basic Facts

A.

$0 \times 4 =$ _____

$1 \times 9 =$ _____

$5 \times 7 =$ _____

$3 \times 4 =$ _____

$2 \times 9 =$ _____

$7 \times 6 =$ _____

B.

$2 \times 5 =$ _____

$6 \times 6 =$ _____

$0 \times 7 =$ _____

$1 \times 3 =$ _____

$8 \times 11 =$ _____

$6 \times 8 =$ _____

C.

$8 \times 0 =$ _____

$4 \times 10 =$ _____

$2 \times 1 =$ _____

$8 \times 8 =$ _____

$9 \times 6 =$ _____

$5 \times 6 =$ _____

Bonus: Circle the **even** answers.
Draw a square around the **odd** number answers.

One-Digit Times Two-Digit Multiplication

Multiply to solve the problems.

A.

21	70	42	76
x 9	x 0	x 3	x 6

B.

98	61	21	22
x 1	x 2	x 4	x 2

C.

64	29	38	56
x 4	x 5	x 7	x 9

Punctuation Review

Add the correct **punctuation** at the end of each sentence.

1. Who won the big football game _____

2. I went to the zoo last week with Tony _____

3. Please pass the salt _____

4. I would like to learn to sew _____

5. I cannot believe he did that _____

6. I can't get out of this tree. Help _____

7. Katie used to live in Texas _____

8. That ladder is going to fall. Look out _____

9. We are going to the lake _____

10. When is Elliott's birthday _____

Sequencing Events

Read the story to learn about the old house. Then, read the sentences below. Decide what happened first, second, and so on. Number the sentences in the correct order.

The Old House

Jerome was the one who discovered the old house in the first place. It was late one day last October. Jerome had taken a shortcut through the woods and there it was! That house was so spooky, it scared him just to look at it.

The next day at school, Jerome told Lisa Peterson. By the time the school day was through, the whole school knew about the house. All of the kids wanted to see it. A group of Jerome's friends planned to meet there right after dinner.

Nearly 20 boys and girls showed up at the house just before 6 o'clock. They walked around the old empty building in a close group.

Suddenly, they all heard a loud shriek. Everyone jumped and some children even screamed. Jerome looked up at one of the window ledges. There sat a big, black crow. All of the children laughed. They had let their imaginations get the best of them. They knew then that the house was not really scary. They all agreed that it had been a fun-filled adventure just the same.

_____ The children walked around the house.

_____ Jerome told Lisa Peterson about the house.

_____ The children knew the house was not scary.

_____ Jerome discovered the old house.

_____ The children saw a crow on a ledge.

_____ Nearly 20 boys and girls showed up at the old house before 6 o'clock.

_____ Some of Jerome's friends planned to meet at the old house after dinner.

One-Digit Times Three-Digit Multiplication

Multiply to solve the problems.

A.   173
     x 3

B.   452
     x 2

C.   168
     x 5

D.   223
     x 6

E.   180
     x 5

F.   232
     x 4

G.   549
     x 2

H.   257
     x 8

Write the answers in order from smallest to largest.

_____ _____ _____ _____ _____ _____ _____ _____

Combining Root Words and Suffixes

Use the suffix bank and the word list to **create as many words as you can**. Write the words on the lines at the bottom of the page. Remember to change the **y** to an **i** when adding a suffix. Use another sheet of paper if needed.

Suffix Bank

-er	-ful	-less
-ly	-ness	

Word List

teach	thought
beauty	boast
doubt	shy
happy	bake
sad	care
quick	friend
awkward	help
peace	law
quiet	wonder

1. _____
2. _____
3. _____
4. _____
5. _____
6. _____
7. _____
8. _____
9. _____
10. _____
11. _____
12. _____
13. _____
14. _____
15. _____
16. _____
17. _____
18. _____
19. _____
20. _____
21. _____
22. _____

Compound Words

Fill in each blank with a word from the word list to make a **compound word**
Use each word only once.

Word List	boat	shore	case	fly	nap	bug
	board	burger	crow	coat	book	time

scare_____   night_____

cook_____   cheese_____

cat_____   sea_____

steam_____   horse_____

suit_____   chalk_____

rain_____   lady_____

Story Problems

Solve each word problem.

A. The Super Coaster roller coaster ride has 15 cars. Each car has 4 seats.
How many people can ride the Super Coaster at one time?

_____

B. Last week, 21 mother dogs had puppies If they each had 6 puppies, how
many puppies did the dogs have altogether? _____

C. Cheri can make 32 bracelets a week. She made bracelets for 12 weeks.
How many bracelets did Cheri make? _____

D. Sixteen packages of crayons were donated to Mr. Horowitz's class. Each
package had 64 crayons. How many crayons were donated in all?

_____

Greater Than or Less Than?

Multiply to solve the problems. Write > or < in the box to show if the first answer is greater or less than the second answer.

A. 159 x 8 ☐ 221 x 5

B. 983 x 3 ☐ 759 x 4

C. 865 x 1 ☐ 182 x 7

D. 135 x 9 ☐ 203 x 5

E. 315 x 4 ☐ 275 x 6

F. 249 x 2 ☐ 259 x 3

Using Synonyms

Read each sentence. Replace the word in parentheses with a **synonym**. Write the synonym on the line.

1. Rascal is a (small) ____________ dog.
2. Timmy can run (fast) ____________.
3. Did you (complete) ____________ your homework?
4. I like to (yell) ____________ when I am outside.
5. That box is an (odd) ____________ color.
6. Will your mother (allow) ____________ us to eat pizza?
7. My father brought me a (present) ____________.
8. Kelly is wearing a (pretty) ____________ dress.
9. Sonja recycled her (ancient) ____________ letters.
10. The cat slept (below) ____________ the table.
11. Patty likes to (converse) ____________ with her friends.

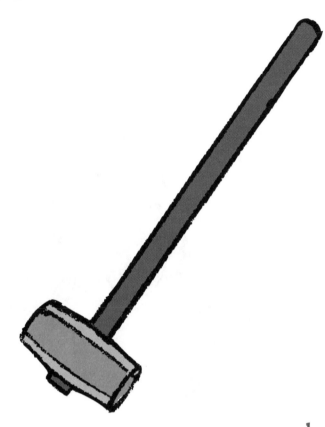

The Steel-Drivin' Man

1

It was called the race of the century—the 19th century, that is. It was a contest of man versus machine, and when it was over, everyone knew the name of Big John Henry.

Back in the days before automobiles and airplanes, before machines did the work of men and women, Big John worked on the railroads in West Virginia, clearing the way for locomotives to steam across the Appalachian Mountains, moving people and goods from coast to coast.

3

John was the biggest, fastest, and strongest man working on the rails. He helped dig a tunnel through a huge mountain named Big Bend. His hammer was 10 feet long and weighed 40 pounds, but he didn't mind. He used it to drive a long steel drill deep into the side of the mountain to clear the way for explosives that blasted away the rock.

The mountain was a mile and a half thick, and the tunnel was deep and dark. Big John Henry worked 12-hour days from sunup to sundown. It was said that John sometimes used two hammers at the same time, one for each arm, which was unheard of in those days. Sometimes, when he swung his hammer down on his drill, the men in the tunnel would run for their lives because they thought the mountain was caving in on them. And Big John would just grin and say, "Sorry, fellas. That's just my hammer you hear sucking in the wind."

2

Now, there were some that thought machines could do a better job on the tunnel than men could, even men like Big John. One day, a salesman wandered into camp with a huge device called a steam drill. He tried to sell it to John's boss, the railroad captain.

When word got to John about this, he rushed over to the captain and cried, "I'll die with a hammer in my hand before I let a machine steal my job from me!"

So the captain made John an offer. John and the other workers could keep their jobs if John raced the steam drill and won. Whoever dug a deeper hole into the side of the mountain within a day would be the winner. Big John didn't hesitate for a moment. He grabbed his hammer and said, "I'll topple this mountain before they can say a machine beat a steel-drivin' man."

4

News of the race spread from town to town, and soon hundreds of people were surrounding the old Big Bend the night before the race. There were people selling food and drink, toy hammers and drills, and even newspapers that read "Big John Battles the Bane of Humanity." No one knew what this meant, but they bought the papers anyway.

John had a good night's rest and ate a hearty meal of two dozen pancakes and a side of ham. By daybreak, he was standing with his hammer in hand by the mouth of the tunnel, ready to teach that machine a lesson.

But the salesman was confident in his steam drill, too. He knew that it would never get tired. It would never slow its pace. It would never need to eat or take a break. And it could drill into rock a whole lot faster than any man could, no matter how big or strong he was. In his opinion, Big John didn't have a chance in the world.

5

But John kept hammering. His pace was steady, and he never missed a stroke. Everyone could see that Big John Henry was true to his word. He would die with a hammer in his hand before he let a machine bring him down.

As the sun set, the whistle blew and the race was finally over. John and the salesman stepped aside as the railroad captain compared the holes they'd made. First, he measured the steam drill's hole. Nine feet! The crowd booed, but the salesman was happy. No man had ever drilled a nine-foot hole into rock in just one day. It was a world record!

Then, the captain went to John's hole. John stood nearby, his hammer still in his hands. The crowd held its breath. The captain placed his measuring tape into the hole and then lifted it out. He turned to the crowd and announced: "Fourteen feet!"

A cheer erupted from the crowd that was so loud, people in Delaware could hear it. Big John Henry had beaten the machine!

7

Soon it was time to begin. The salesman moved the steam drill into position by a wall of rock. John Henry lifted his hammer and stood next to it. The crowd fell silent as the railroad captain lifted his starting gun into the air. On the count of three, he fired a shot. The race had begun!

Some say that when the race started, flames burst from Big John's hammer when it struck a blow. Others claim that the thunderous sound that came from every stroke knocked the people nearby clean off their feet.

The salesman's steam drill was equally impressive. With hardly any effort at all, the machine plowed through the thick rock wall. In just a few minutes, a cloud of dust and debris spread over the sky and blocked out the sun.

As the day passed, the shadows got smaller and then longer again. Big John was standing ankle-deep in a pool of perspiration, and you could see the veins bulging in his massive forearms. You could tell that the hammer was growing heavy in his hands. But the machine next to him showed no signs of slowing down. People were starting to worry about Big John. They wondered how long he could keep this up.

6

Everyone was so happy that no one noticed when John laid his huge hammer on the ground or when he sat down next to it with his back against the mountain. Big John Henry had proven that a person was better than a machine any day, but he would not live to see the end of this one. He died with a big grin on his face and his hammer at his side.

Nowadays, machines make all of our lives easier, but no one will ever forget the day John Henry beat that steam drill. And some days, when the wind is blowing just right, you can still hear his hammer ring.

8

Synonym Search

Match each pair of synonyms in the box below by connecting a word from the first column to a word in the second column. Then, find and circle each synonym pair in the word search. (*Hint:* Each pair of words is spelled across or down and does not share any letters.)

```
C H O O S E S E L E C T   C B Y
Z W X E C R V T B Y N I   N B Y P
E Q U I C K F A S T C D N A Q V E
R C R V T B Y N U A S D Y A V S R I T
R J O Y O U S M E R T B Y T G T N E J E
R C R G E C O M U R Y B B S E A R B I N
M K C E A W D X Z M U V T G V L R B V Y
I C E N W D E X Q R A E R F G E A C V B
S C N W S S X Z X D S E R F G A L Y N N
T V U I Q A Z T U O F V S K H F N L T B
A D N N Q E X C D A C T V G B F R Y W N
K V E Q S X T U F R H B J N A L E X B B
E D R R A S H A C I T H A M R D T F N E
W C E B E G I R D C N S U Y O L E X F N
A C A W C T B D T R V C W Y L M A F C E
S V L W T B D C T R I G H T A F D X V
C O R R E C T U I P L M H F D X
X E C R T U I P L M H F D X C V
```

decay	nearly
error	rot
quick	mistake
almost	fast
joyous	start
genuine	select
correct	merry
petite	real
choose	right
begin	tiny

Interpreting a Grid

The children in Mr. Price's class made a **grid** showing the pets they own. Each check mark stands for one pet owned by a child. Use the grid to answer the questions.

Pets Owned by Mr. Price's Students

	Keisha	Juan	Maria	Tim	Anthony
turtle		√			√
rabbit	√	√			
snake	√				
lizard			√	√	
mouse	√	√			
fish		√	√	√	
cat	√	√	√	√	√
dog	√	√	√		√

A. What is the total number of pets listed on the grid? _____

B. Which child owns the most pets? _____

C. Which type of pet is owned by every child? _____

D. How many children own turtles? _____

E. How many more pets does Maria have than Tim? _____

F. Does Anthony have a pet turtle? _____ a rabbit? _____

G. What pets does Juan not own? _____

Finish the Sentences

Read each sentence. Using the word list below, fill in each blank with a word that means the same as the highlighted word in each sentence.

Word List

totally	increase
absent	uncomfortable
detest	strange
talented	remain
error	companion

1. Kim was **missing** from school today because she was _____ .

2. I **hate** ketchup and I _____ mustard, so I ate my hamburger plain.

3. Beside being a **gifted** musician, he is a _____ artist.

4. Mother told us to **stay** in this area, so we'd better _____ here until she returns.

5. I have this **miserable** head cold, and I've felt _____ all day.

6. That's **peculiar**; I've never heard that _____ noise before.

7. I made another **mistake** on my math paper! That's the third _____ I've made today.

8. Jane is a good **friend**, and no one could ask for a better _____ .

9. He hopes that his plants will **multiply** and _____ his earnings.

10. I was **completely** covered with mud, and my clothes were _____ ruined.

Show Your Work

Multiply to solve each problem.

A.   853
    x 25
	B. 657
	    x 61
		C. 574
		    x 80

D.   286
    x 51
	E. 125
	    x 97
		F. 913
		    x 64

Forming Plurals with y

Complete each sentence with the **plural** form of a noun from the box below.

bunny	day	family	key	party	penny	strawberry

1. There are only ten more _____ until school starts.

2. Grandmother used many _____ to make the pie.

3. Sandra needed a few more _____ to buy the comic book.

4. It takes two _____ to unlock our front door.

5. My pet rabbit gave birth to three baby _____ .

6. I have been to two birthday _____ this week.

7. There were _____ in line at the grocery store.

Forming Plurals with f

Rewrite each word in the box as a **plural** on the line.

1. I would like to buy three _____ of bread.

2. Place the encyclopedias on those _____ .

3. The _____ stood close to their mothers.

4. The _____ were hunting for food.

5. We wore our _____ outside in the snow.

6. A whole is made up of two _____ .

loaf
shelf
calf
wolf
scarf
half

Show Your Work Again

Math

Multiply to solve each problem.

525	917	816
x 51	x 22	x 87

950	835	727
x 16	x 10	x 31

What's Wrong?

Read each paragraph. Underline the sentence in each paragraph that **does not belong**. The first one has been done for you.

1. Martha's dad is an electrician. He does many different kinds of things when he goes to work. Some days he checks the wiring in peoples' homes. Sometimes he checks the wiring in large buildings and shopping centers. <u>Martha is very proud of him.</u> He often helps put all the electrical wires and outlets in new buildings.

2. Jeremy has many reasons for wanting to be a dentist. He thinks having healthy teeth is very important. He has always been interested in all the things his own dentist does. Jeremy thinks he would be a good dentist, too. He has always enjoyed school.

3. Being a florist takes special training. You must know the names of all the flowers and plants. People who are in the hospital like to receive flowers. You must learn how to care for flowers and plants. It is also important to know how to arrange them.

4. Carl wants to be a teacher, but he can't decide what to teach. At first, he thought he would like to teach math. Then, he thought he would like to teach kindergarten. Carl likes many things. Now he thinks he would like to teach history.

How Much Money?

Calculate the money in each piggy bank and print the total on the line.
Use a dollar sign and a decimal point for each amount.

A.
2 dimes
4 pennies
5 quarters
_____

B.
5 nickels
6 dimes
2 quarters
_____

C.
8 quarters
2 dimes
68 pennies
_____

D.
5 pennies
12 dimes
10 nickels
_____

Contraction Fun

Rewrite the words below as **contractions**. Use the key to create a patchwork design pattern at the bottom of the page.

1. she will _____
2. you are _____
3. he would _____
4. there is _____
5. I am _____
6. can not _____
7. they are _____
8. should not _____
9. what is _____
10. they will _____
11. we would _____
12. we are _____

If the word ends in	Draw this pattern in the grid
'll	
're	
'd	
's	
'm	
't	

1.	2.	3.	4.
5.	6.	7.	8.
9.	10.	11.	12.

Solve the Code

Multiply and solve the code to find out who wins the race.
Use a calculator.

J	W	N	I
169	512	774	907
x 417	x 692	x 523	x 830

N	O	A	S
825	382	306	614
x 504	x 379	x 168	x 452

_____ _____ _____ _____   _____ _____ _____ _____

70,473   144,778   51,408   404,802   354,304   752,810   415,800   277,528

Prefixes

Choose the correct **prefixes** to form new words below. Write the prefix on the blank in front of each word. Color each box the color listed next to each prefix you choose.

pre – (color red)   **un** – (color blue)   **mis** – (color yellow)   **re** – (color green)

1. ☐ _____lead

2. ☐ _____tend

3. ☐ _____tell

4. ☐ _____fix

5. ☐ _____fair

6. ☐ _____happy

7. ☐ _____flex

8. ☐ ___conduct

9. ☐ _____fill

Analogies

Compare the relationships of the words below.
Find the missing word for each analogy and write it in the space provided.

1. in : out : : up : _____
2. two : four : : three : _____
3. snow : cold : : sun : _____
4. mother : aunt : : father : _____
5. ear : hear : : eye : _____
6. she : her : : he : _____
7. dog : bark : : bird : _____
8. brother : boy : : sister : _____
9. bear : den : : bee : _____
10. finger : hand : : toe : _____
11. girl : mother : : boy : _____
12. left : right : : top : _____

Learning to Divide

Math

Divide to solve each problem.

A. $4\overline{)32}$ B. $2\overline{)10}$

C. $5\overline{)45}$ D. $2\overline{)18}$

E. $7\overline{)35}$ F. $6\overline{)54}$ G. $2\overline{)12}$ H. $3\overline{)36}$

Division Designs

Divide. Then connect the dots in order, beginning with the number given first.

Start at 5.

A. 45 ÷ _____ = 5
B. 12 ÷ _____ = 6
C. 36 ÷ _____ = 6
D. 6 ÷ _____ = 2
E. 8 ÷ _____ = 1
F. 35 ÷ _____ = 7
G. 7 ÷ _____ = 1

H. 24 ÷ _____ = 8
I. 42 ÷ _____ = 7
J. 6 ÷ _____ = 3
K. 27 ÷ _____ = 3
L. 2 ÷ _____ = 2
M. 54 ÷ _____ = 9

Start at 6.

A. 18 ÷ _____ = 6
B. 20 ÷ _____ = 5
C. 10 ÷ _____ = 2
D. 24 ÷ _____ = 4
E. 14 ÷ _____ = 7
F. 64 ÷ _____ = 8

G. 5 ÷ _____ = 1
H. 48 ÷ _____ = 6
I. 9 ÷ _____ = 1
J. 42 ÷ _____ = 6
K. 2 ÷ _____ = 1

Linking Verbs

A **linking verb** does not show action but shows a state of being. It connects the subject of a sentence to a word or phrase that describes or renames the subject. Linking verbs include forms of **to be**, such as **am**, **is**, **are**, **was**, and **were**.

Example: The cow **was** black and white.

Read each sentence. Circle the linking verb.

1. Mary was happy when so many people attended her dance recital.

2. Kelsey is sorry she missed the party.

3. Mysteries are my favorite type of book!

4. Today is January third.

5. We were pleased to see our team win the game.

6. Kay was amused when Ken told jokes.

7. I am anxious to finish my homework before dinner.

8. Mr. Alton was quiet during the concert.

Identifying Parts of Speech

Read each sentence. Decide if the highlighted word is an **adjective**, an **adverb**, a **noun,** or a **verb**. Use the key to write **Adj**, **Adv**, **N**, or **V** on the line.

Key			
Adj – adjective	**Adv – adverb**	**N – noun**	**V – verb**

_____ 1. The **big**, red apple fell off the tree.

_____ 2. The yellow **dog** followed Trina.

_____ 3. Sarah **fell** down the stairs.

_____ 4. **Broccoli** is on sale at the market today.

_____ 5. Kenny **slowly** walked to school.

_____ 6. My **new** sweater is very warm.

_____ 7. Mariah **sprinted** across the meadow.

_____ 8. The **winner** of the race cried tears of joy.

_____ 9. The **tornado** did not damage any homes.

Story Problems

Solve the story problems.

A. Patricia bought 16 doughnuts for herself and her 3 friends. If they each eat the same number of doughnuts, how many will each person eat?

_____

B. Catherine has 7 days to knit 21 sweaters. If she knits the same number of sweaters each day, how many will she have to make each day?

_____

C. Victoria picked 72 apples and used them to make pies. She used 6 apples in each pie. How many pies did Victoria make?

_____

Descriptive Writing

Read the short paragraph.

It was a nice day. Without warning, a storm suddenly blew in over the lake. We were afraid our boat would sink.

Here are some adjectives that can help describe the sentences:

What kind of day it was: bright, sunny, lovely, warm, spring

How the storm came in: quickly, gusting, swirling, howling, thundering, booming

What the storm looked like: dark, cloudy, windy, blackness, inky

What the people looked like: pale, tense, worried, frightened

Rewrite the paragraph to make it more colorful and interesting. Use the adjectives above or think of your own to describe what has happened in the paragraph. Give the paragraph a title.

_____

_____

_____

_____

_____

_____

_____

_____

_____

_____

Beat the Clock (Division Facts 0 to 9)

A.	36 ÷ 6 =	8 ÷ 1 =	45 ÷ 9 =	16 ÷ 8 =	35 ÷ 5 =
B.	24 ÷ 8 =	27 ÷ 9 =	20 ÷ 5 =	21 ÷ 3 =	8 ÷ 2 =
C.	20 ÷ 4 =	42 ÷ 7 =	18 ÷ 6 =	14 ÷ 2 =	28 ÷ 7 =
D.	56 ÷ 8 =	9 ÷ 3 =	3 ÷ 1 =	40 ÷ 8 =	12 ÷ 4 =
E.	10 ÷ 2 =	48 ÷ 6 =	45 ÷ 5 =	0 ÷ 6 =	15 ÷ 3 =
F.	7 ÷ 7 =	6 ÷ 2 =	18 ÷ 9 =	7 ÷ 1 =	32 ÷ 4 =
G.	5 ÷ 1 =	35 ÷ 5 =	56 ÷ 7 =	5 ÷ 5 =	30 ÷ 3 =
H.	18 ÷ 6 =	15 ÷ 5 =	18 ÷ 2 =	72 ÷ 8 =	2 ÷ 1 =
I.	30 ÷ 5 =	1 ÷ 1 =	21 ÷ 7 =	8 ÷ 4 =	0 ÷ 3 =
J.	9 ÷ 9 =	28 ÷ 4 =	16 ÷ 4 =	12 ÷ 2 =	36 ÷ 9 =
K.	8 ÷ 8 =	27 ÷ 3 =	6 ÷ 6 =	6 ÷ 3 =	0 ÷ 4 =
L.	12 ÷ 3 =	81 ÷ 9 =	0 ÷ 2 =	49 ÷ 7 =	36 ÷ 9 =
M.	30 ÷ 6 =	32 ÷ 8 =	9 ÷ 1 =	0 ÷ 8 =	14 ÷ 7 =
N.	35 ÷ 7 =	16 ÷ 2 =	0 ÷ 7 =	42 ÷ 6 =	6 ÷ 1 =
O.	45 ÷ 9 =	24 ÷ 4 =	10 ÷ 5 =	0 ÷ 1 =	12 ÷ 6 =
P.	2 ÷ 2 =	0 ÷ 5 =	24 ÷ 6 =	40 ÷ 5 =	24 ÷ 3 =
Q.	54 ÷ 6 =	27 ÷ 9 =	18 ÷ 3 =	25 ÷ 5 =	63 ÷ 9 =
R.	64 ÷ 8 =	4 ÷ 1 =	4 ÷ 4 =	0 ÷ 9 =	4 ÷ 2 =
S.	72 ÷ 8 =	63 ÷ 7 =	48 ÷ 8 =	27 ÷ 9 =	24 ÷ 8 =
T.	36 ÷ 4 =	54 ÷ 9 =	3 ÷ 3 =	40 ÷ 5 =	14 ÷ 7 =

Time: **Number correct:**

Sentences & Fragments

Read each group of words. If the group is only a fragment, write **F** on the line. If it is a sentence, write **S** on the line and add the correct ending punctuation. The first one has been done for you.

___**S**___ **1.** Isabelle is a good dancer .

_____ **2.** To the park

_____ **3.** Ride in the car

_____ **4.** Be careful

_____ **5.** Stacey liked the movie

_____ **6.** Will you come over tomorrow

_____ **7.** On top of the house by the chimney

_____ **8.** With Tina and Gina

Division Designs

Fill in the missing **divisors**. Then, connect the dots in order, beginning with the number given first.

Start at 6.

A. $30 \div \_\_\_\_ = 6$

B. $15 \div \_\_\_\_ = 5$

C. $28 \div \_\_\_\_ = 4$

D. $20 \div \_\_\_\_ = 4$

E. $9 \div \_\_\_\_ = 9$

F. $56 \div \_\_\_\_ = 8$

G. $6 \div \_\_\_\_ = 1$

H. $21 \div \_\_\_\_ = 7$

I. $40 \div \_\_\_\_ = 5$

J. $48 \div \_\_\_\_ = 8$

Start at 2.

A. $5 \div \_\_\_\_ = 5$

B. $63 \div \_\_\_\_ = 9$

C. $9 \div \_\_\_\_ = 3$

D. $8 \div \_\_\_\_ = 4$

E. $18 \div \_\_\_\_ = 3$

F. $56 \div \_\_\_\_ = 7$

G. $45 \div \_\_\_\_ = 9$

H. $12 \div \_\_\_\_ = 4$

I. $21 \div \_\_\_\_ = 3$

J. $63 \div \_\_\_\_ = 7$

K. $25 \div \_\_\_\_ = 5$

Complete Subjects

Draw a line under the **complete subject** of each sentence below.

1. Astronauts are very brave people.
2. Donna's birthday is today.
3. The big, red boat sped across the water.
4. The spectators enjoyed the fireworks.
5. Barbara and Cindy love to garden.
6. The blue engine stopped at the station.
7. The actor was excellent in the play.
8. The movie was the best one I have ever seen!
9. Good health is important to everyone.
10. All children love to play.
11. The pictures in that book are beautiful.
12. The raft floated across the lake.

>, =, or <

Divide to solve each problem. Write **>**, **=**, or **<** to compare the answers.

A. $5\overline{)25}$ B. $7\overline{)35}$

C. $3\overline{)27}$ D. $4\overline{)32}$

E. $8\overline{)56}$ F. $7\overline{)49}$

G. $2\overline{)18}$ H. $9\overline{)36}$

A ☐ F

D ☐ B

C ☐ G

E ☐ H

Division Practice

Divide to solve each problem.

A. $4\overline{)24}$ B. $9\overline{)72}$ C. $4\overline{)36}$ D. $7\overline{)70}$

E. $2\overline{)12}$ F. $4\overline{)16}$

G. $2\overline{)20}$ H. $3\overline{)21}$

Conjunctions

Select the correct **conjunction** to complete each sentence. Write it on the line.

and	but	or

1. I have enough money to buy both a ball _____ a bat.

2. You may have either milk _____ juice to drink.

3. Her favorite sandwich is peanut butter _____ jelly.

4. John took swimming lessons, _____ he still could not swim.

5. Mom said I can choose either pancakes _____ waffles.

6. We will go either to the mountains _____ the ocean on our vacation.

7. The United States' flag is red, white, _____ blue.

8. Johnny worked very hard on his report, _____ he only made a B.

Understanding What I've Read

Independence Day

The Fourth of July is an important holiday for the United States. It is Independence Day. On July 4, 1776, the United States declared, or stated, that it was a country. It would no longer be part of England. "Independence" means to take care of yourself without help from others. That is why July 4 is called Independence Day. Every Fourth of July people in the United States celebrate the beginning of the country. There are parades, speeches, and lots of fireworks. People fly their flags to show they are proud of their country.

1. What is the main idea of this story?
   a. The founding of the United States is celebrated on July 4.
   b. Parades are common on July 4.
   c. July 4 is for fireworks.

2. On what day does the United States celebrate its independence?

   _____

3. What word means **to state or say**?
   a. declare
   b. celebrate
   c. fireworks

4. What are some ways people celebrate Independence Day?

   _____

   _____

5. From whom did the United States declare its independence?

   _____

6. What does the word **independent** mean?
   a. holiday
   b. stated
   c. free and on your own

Division

Divide to solve each problem.

A. 56 ÷ 7 = _____   B. 24 ÷ 8 = _____   C. 54 ÷ 9 = _____

D. 32 ÷ 8 = _____   E. 12 ÷ 3 = _____   F. 25 ÷ 5 = _____

G. 50 ÷ 5 = _____   H. 42 ÷ 7 = _____   I. 72 ÷ 9 = _____

J. 66 ÷ 6 = _____   K. 40 ÷ 5 = _____   L. 21 ÷ 3 = _____

Main Idea

The **main idea** of a paragraph is its central thought or topic. Read each paragraph and the three phrases below it. Decide which one tells the main idea. Write the letter of that phrase on the line.

_____ 1. Taffy's little brother was missing again. At least, no one knew where he was. Little Jeff could get into the strangest places. He would stay hidden until everyone got worried or mad. His favorite place to hide was in the clothes hamper. Taffy's mother said they should put a bell on Jeff!

   a. A mischievous boy   **b.** The clothes hamper   **c.** Taffy's family

_____ 2. Waterskiing is a lot of fun once you learn how. Sailing and boating are nice ways to spend a summer day. Water polo is fun to play. If you are near the ocean, bodysurfing and windsurfing are really exciting.

   a. Summertime   **b.** Water sports   **c.** Waterskiing

_____ 3. Ted asked his dad if he could have an allowance. Ted's dad said that he certainly could! He also said that Ted would have to do a few chores around the house. That was how he would earn his allowance. Every week Ted had to mow the lawn. He also had to take out the garbage. Ted had only been earning an allowance for three weeks. He was already thinking of asking for a raise!

   a. Cleaning the garage   **b.** Ted and his dad   **c.** Earning an allowance

Writing Sentences

Read each pair of sentences. Rewrite the facts in a single sentence on the line.

1. Anna went to the beach. Anna wore her new bathing suit.

   _____

2. Billy hit a home run. Billy's team voted him the player of the game.

   _____

3. Charlie fell down the steps. Charlie was embarrassed.

   _____

4. Dianne went to the mall. Dianne bought a pair of jeans.

   _____

5. Eric painted a picture. Eric got paint on the floor.

   _____

6. Fran went to Gina's house. Fran and Gina played games.

   _____

Division Facts

 Math

Divide to solve each problem.

A. 63 ⎯ 9 = _____

B. 49 ÷ 7 = _____

C. 15 ÷ 3 = _____

D. 64 ÷ 8 _____

E. 30 ÷ 6 = _____

F. 80 ÷ 8 = _____

G. 12 ÷ 2 = _____

H. 45 ÷ 5 = _____

I. 81 ÷ 9 = _____

Magic Trail

Follow the trail by solving the math problems. Can you find the magic number?

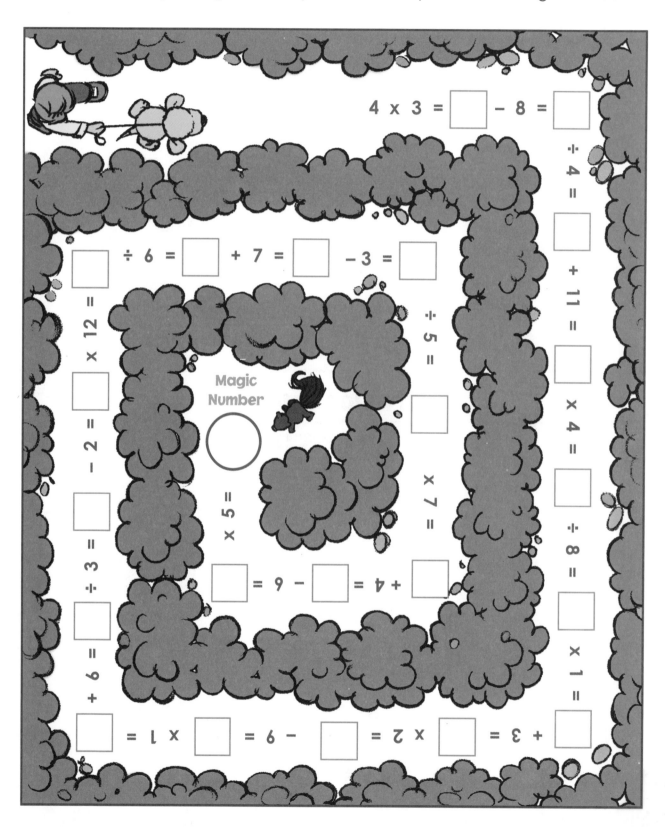

Constructing Stories

Create a short story by answering the questions about the picture.
Use adjectives for description.

1. Who or what is this story about?

_____

2. Where does this story take place?

_____

3. How does this story begin?

_____

4. What will happen next? _____

_____

5. How will the story end? _____

_____

Write a short story using the information above. Be sure to use capital letters and periods.
Remember to indent the first sentence and give your story a title.

_____

_____

_____

_____

_____

_____

Division with Remainders

Divide to solve each problem.

A. $7\overline{)52}$ B. $9\overline{)83}$ C. $6\overline{)40}$ D. $5\overline{)29}$

E. $9\overline{)42}$ F. $3\overline{)55}$ G. $5\overline{)27}$ H. $2\overline{)37}$

Using Suffixes

Look at each word below. Write the **suffix** from the box that makes sense with the word on the line. Note that some words may have more than one possible answer.

er	ful	less	ly	ness

1. paint_____   2. mouth_____   3. sorrow_____

4. bowl_____   5. teach_____   6. shy_____

7. event_____   8. harm_____   9. quick_____

10. care_____   11. will_____

12. motion_____   13. coward_____

14. cheer_____   15. loud_____

16. nice_____   17. help_____

18. price_____

Word Box Stories

Write eight words about the picture in the word box. Use the words to write a story. Be sure to use adjectives, capital letters, and periods. Give your story a title.

Things to Think About

Who is this story about?   Where does this story take place?

How does this story begin?   What happens next?

How will this story end?

Word Box

_____   _____

_____   _____

_____   _____

_____   _____

_____

_____
_____
_____
_____
_____
_____
_____
_____

Root Words

Look at each word below. Write each **root word** on the line.

1. nonsense

2. rewrite

3. spoonful

4. happiness

_____   _____   _____   _____

5. kindness

6. brotherhood

7. ticklish

8. quickly

_____   _____   _____   _____

q. baker

10. lovable

11. helpless

12. cleanness

_____   _____   _____   _____

Three–Digit Dividends

Math

Divide to solve each problem.

A. $5\overline{)125}$

B. $6\overline{)468}$

C. $4\overline{)632}$

D. $9\overline{)945}$

E. $8\overline{)704}$

F. $2\overline{)778}$

G. $7\overline{)672}$

H. $7\overline{)784}$

Predicates

The **simple predicate** is a verb that tells what the subject did or what was done to the subject. The **complete predicate** includes the verb and all the words that tell more about it.

Example: The white cat slept on the pillow.

The simple predicate is **slept** and the complete predicate is **slept on the pillow**.

Underline the complete predicate of each sentence. Circle the simple predicate.

1. Bess danced in the school play.
2. We went to the mall after the library.
3. California is a state on the West Coast.
4. The weather began to turn cool.
5. It rained for hours yesterday!
6. Opal made a painting for her mom.
7. Snow fell for six hours.
8. Seven students were in the spelling bee.
9. The tractor made a loud noise.
10. We served ice cream and cake at the party.

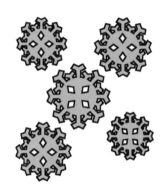

Word Problems with Division

Read the word problems below. Solve each problem.

A. Jim, Steve, and Earl chartered a fishing boat. The trip cost $36. The men divided the cost of the trip between them equally. How much did each man have to pay? $ _____

B. Jen has 21 dolls. If she puts the same number of dolls in 3 different doll houses, how many dolls will she put in each house?

_____ dolls

C. Mabel had a dinner party for her friends. She prpared 24 meals and set up 4 tables. She wanted the same number of people at each table. How many people did she put at each table?

_____ people

Main Idea

Circle or write the **main idea** of each paragraph.

1.   It is September. It is the night of the first football game of the year. Everyone at Kidwell School is excited. Most excited of all is Cliff. This is the very first night he has ever marched with the band. He holds his clarinet nervously. As the director's white glove raises up, Cliff's heart skips a beat. He has dreamed of this moment and it is finally here. He is a member of the marching band.

   a. Cliff's first football game as a band member
   b. Excitement on the night of the first game
   c. Cliff and his friends at the football game

2.   There are many different eyeglass frames. Some are very large. Some are simple and some are fancy. Carol liked every pair she chose. Her favorite pair looked like blue ovals.

   The main idea is: _____

Money Word Problems

Math

Solve each word problem.

A.   Joe and Sam earned $24 raking leaves. They divided the money evenly between them. How much did each person get?

$ _____

B.   Mrs Smith made 12 tacos. She gave her 4 children an equal number of tacos. How many tacos did each child receive?

_____ tacos

C.   Jamie and Eddie bought a pack of art paper. The pack contained 20 pieces of paper. If they each take the same amount of paper, how many pieces will they each get?

_____ pieces

D.   Randi has a package of candy containing 49 pieces. If she wanted to eat an equal share of the candy every day for 7 days, how many pieces would she eat each day?

_____ pieces

The American Heroine

1

Deborah was born in Plympton, Massachusetts, in 1760. Her family was very poor. They sent her to live as a servant with the Thomas family where she took care of their 10 sons. She worked hard on the Thomas farm. When she did her chores, she wore men's clothing since it was easier than wearing a long dress. Deborah was not sent to school, so she taught herself to read and write at night.

By the age of 18, Deborah had grown to be five feet eight inches tall, which was very tall for that time period. She was very strong, too, from years of farm work. But Deborah decided to give up life on the farm. Instead, she became a schoolteacher and taught students in a one-room schoolhouse. At night, she listened to stories men told of the war against England.

3

Many brave soldiers fought in the American Revolutionary War. Frank Shurtliff was one of them. He was severely wounded in battle, yet he returned to keep fighting. His fellow soldiers admired him. Little did they know, Frank was really a woman in disguise.

Have you ever been told that you couldn't do something, but you went ahead and did it anyway? That is exactly what Deborah Samson did back in 1782. She changed her identity to a man. Then, she joined the American Army to fight against the British.

In those days, women were not allowed to become soldiers. The only way for Deborah to fight for her country was to pretend to be a man. It was a dangerous thing to do, but she felt it was her patriotic duty to face the British on the front lines.

2

For a long time, the American colonists had been upset with the way the British were treating them. They felt they were unfairly taxed and didn't have the right to vote on what happened in their own towns and cities. They couldn't speak freely and British soldiers often stayed in their homes uninvited.

Then, the Americans signed the Declaration of Independence and the country went to war with England. Many of the men Deborah knew were joining the army to fight. Deborah was angry with what the British were doing, too. She also wanted to help free her country. It wasn't fair that they wouldn't let her become a soldier just because she was a woman. Deborah decided to do her duty anyway.

4

Deborah disguised herself as a man by cutting her hair and wearing men's clothes. At first, she signed the papers to join and then changed her mind. But after a little while, she gathered up her courage and tried again. This time, it worked. She signed her name as Frank Shurtliff and no one suspected that she was really a woman. Her disguise worked. Deborah Samson had become a soldier.

Just three days later, Deborah, now known as Frank, had a uniform and orders to march.

5

Deborah Samson was awarded an Honorable Discharge from the military. She returned home to her family in Massachusetts. Soon after, the Americans won the war.

Two years later, Deborah married a farmer named Benjamin Gannett. They had three children but were very poor. Her friend Paul Revere, the famous messenger of the war, helped her receive the money she was owed for fighting in the army. Then, once Deborah's story started to spread, people paid to hear her tell stories about her adventures. Everyone knew her as "the American Heroine."

7

By 1782, the war was almost over, but there was still a lot of fighting going on in the state of New York. Most of the combat was very dangerous. Deborah fought bravely in several of these battles. The other soldiers saw that she was a very strong and courageous warrior. They were honored to serve with her in battle.

Then, Deborah was wounded when her unit was ambushed by enemy troops. She received injuries to the head and leg. She was afraid that the doctor would discover that she was really a woman, so she limped away from the hospital when the doctor wasn't looking. Then, she treated her wounds herself.

Shortly afterwards, Deborah returned to battle. She continued to fight until she collapsed one day with a brain fever. This time, the doctor who found her was surprised to find that Frank Shurtliff was really a woman in disguise.

6

In 1983, 200 years after she fought to defend her country, Deborah Samson was named the "Official Heroine of the Commonwealth of Massachusetts." This was the first time an award like this was given to anyone in the United States. A statue was also erected for Deborah in her hometown.

Because of women like Deborah Samson and their willingness to take chances for what they believed, women now serve as soldiers and are a proud part of the United States Armed Forces. Deborah's heroics and bravery will not be forgotten.

8

Identifying Misspelled Words

Underline the spelling error in each sentence.
Write the correct spelling on the line.

1. Missy tripped while she was runing. _____

2. Do you beleeve that story? _____

3. Valentine's Day is in Febuary. _____

4. I take gymnastics classes on Wensdays. _____

5. Mother made apple pie for desert. _____

6. I like to walk to scool. _____

7. Sara is going to the beech on Saturday. _____

8. It is cool outside, so I will wear a sweter. _____

Adding Fractions

Math

Add the fractions.

A. $\dfrac{5}{8}$
$+ \dfrac{2}{8}$

B. $\dfrac{4}{9}$
$+ \dfrac{3}{9}$

C. $\dfrac{9}{12}$
$+ \dfrac{1}{12}$

D. $\dfrac{1}{6}$
$+ \dfrac{4}{6}$

E. $\dfrac{2}{5}$
$+ \dfrac{3}{5}$

F. $\dfrac{2}{4}$
$+ \dfrac{1}{4}$

G. $\dfrac{3}{5}$
$+ \dfrac{1}{5}$

H. $\dfrac{1}{6}$
$+ \dfrac{4}{6}$

Words into Math

Use the table to answer the questions.
If the information needed to answer a question is not given, write **NG**.

Daily Schedule	Time
Homeroom	8:00 – 8:10
1st Period	8:15 – 9:15
2nd Period	9:20 – 10:25
3rd Period	10:25 – 11:25
Lunch	11:25 – 12:00
4th Period	12:00 – 1:15
5th Period	1:05 – 2:05
6th Period	2:10 – 3:10

Charles High School has this daily schedule. It names all the class periods and gives the time each one starts and ends.

1. How long is each class period?

_____

2. If Jimmy gets to class at 8:30, how much of 1st period has he missed?

_____

3. What class does Susan have 4th period?

_____

4. Kaitlin's mom picked her up at 2:00. During what period did she leave?

_____

5. Jamal stays in Mr. Wood's room for 2nd and 3rd periods. How long is he in that room?

_____

6. During what period does Ms. Smith teach gym?

_____

7. How long is the lunch period?

_____

8. Which period begins at 9:20?

_____

9. What event happens between 8:00 and 8:10 each morning?

_____

10. If school is over after 6th period, what time do the students get out?

_____

Story Web

Finish the story web. Use the words in the web to write a story.
Be sure to use capital letters and periods. Give your story a title.

THINGS TO THINK ABOUT

Who is this story about?   Where does this story take place?

How does this story begin?   What happens next?

How will this story end?

feet		spaceship

trolley	transportation	bicycle

_____

_____

_____

_____

_____

_____

_____

_____

Division Facts 9–12 Review

Divide to solve each problem.

A.
$9\overline{)90}$

B.
$10\overline{)20}$

C.
$11\overline{)99}$

D.
$12\overline{)108}$

E.
$11\overline{)77}$

F.
$12\overline{)24}$

G.
$10\overline{)60}$

H.
$12\overline{)60}$

I.
$11\overline{)110}$

J.
$10\overline{)100}$

K.
$9\overline{)27}$

L.
$9\overline{)9}$

M.
$10\overline{)120}$

N.
$11\overline{)121}$

O.
$9\overline{)108}$

Topic Sentence

A **topic sentence** is a sentence in a paragraph that tells the main idea.

Example: **Ellen disliked all types of tiny, crawling things.** Spiders made her crazy. Worms gave her the willies. Little, shiny lizards made Ellen feel awful. The only tiny, crawling thing Ellen liked was her little brother Ned.

Read each paragraph. Underline the topic sentence.

1.   Raccoons sleep all day. They wake up at night to get food when they are hungry. Fireflies blink on and off at night. Owls hunt for their food after the sun goes down. Bats search for insects after dark. These are all night creatures.

2.   There are many interesting things at the hairstyling shop. There is the stylist's chair that spins around and goes up and down. There are all the different combs, lotions, and special things the stylist uses. Some people like the magazines in the waiting area. Some folks like the hair styles they get the best!

3.   The takeoff was surprisingly smooth. The sky was clear and there were only a few clouds. The flight attendants were all very friendly. Amanda thought her dinner on the plane was delicious. In fact, everything about Amanda's first airplane ride was perfect.

Math Puzzle

Solve the problems below and write the answers in the boxes.
On the building, shade in the squares that match your answers.
The answers will make a pattern.

5 x 3 – 6 = ☐

27 ÷ 3 + 4 = ☐

3 x 6 ÷ 9 = ☐

120 ÷ 10 x 11 = ☐

32 ÷ 8 + 7 = ☐

4 x 3 – 9 = ☐

2 x 3 x 5 = ☐

21 ÷ 7 + 4 = ☐

81 ÷ 9 + 8 = ☐

3 x 2 + 8 = ☐

40 ÷ 5 + 8 = ☐

56 ÷ 7 + 7 = ☐

5 x 8 ÷ 10 = ☐

4 x 9 ÷ 3 = ☐

2 x 9 ÷ 3 = ☐

33 ÷ 3 – 6 = ☐

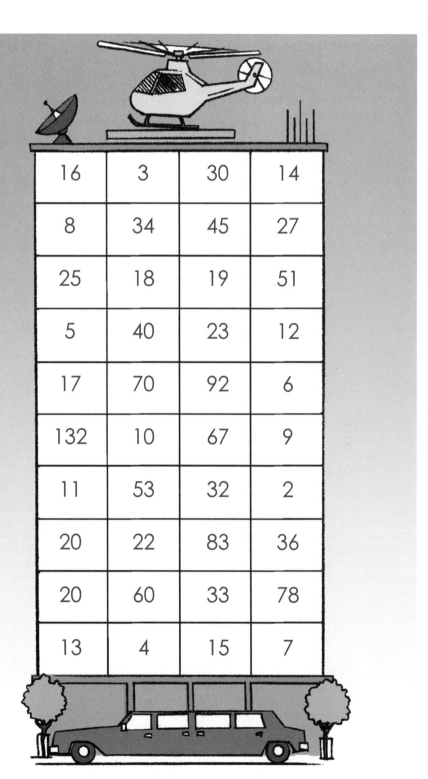

16	3	30	14
8	34	45	27
25	18	19	51
5	40	23	12
17	70	92	6
132	10	67	9
11	53	32	2
20	22	83	36
20	60	33	78
13	4	15	7

Constructing Stories

Things to Think About for Every Story

- Every sentence begins with a capital letter and ends with a period, question mark, or exclamation mark.
- A paragraph contains a main idea and supporting details.
- The first line of a paragraph should be indented.
- Adjectives make stories more colorful and interesting.
- A story tells who did what, when, where, how, and why.
- Stories have a beginning, a middle, and an end.

Write a story about performing on stage. Be sure to follow all of the tips provided. Remember to indent the first sentence of each paragraph and give your story a title.

_____

Solve the Code

You must solve the code to find the alligator's name and cross the stream.
For each answer in the code, write the letter of the corresponding problem.

N
$$4\overline{)933}$$

E
$$8\overline{)930}$$

N
$$5\overline{)732}$$

I
$$3\overline{)913}$$

D
$$9\overline{)994}$$

M
$$6\overline{)980}$$

A
$$5\overline{)844}$$

S
$$2\overline{)827}$$

H
$$9\overline{)933}$$

W
$$7\overline{)802}$$

S
$$7\overline{)934}$$

I
$$3\overline{)503}$$

E
$$6\overline{)759}$$

R
$$8\overline{)981}$$

A
$$4\overline{)694}$$

___ ___ ___   ___ ___ ___ ___
103 R6 304 R1 133 R3   233 R1 173 R2 163 R2 126 R3

___ ___
167 R2 413 R1

___ ___ ___ ___ ___ ___ .
168 R4 146 R2 110 R4 122 R5 116 R2 114 R4

Topic Sentence

A **topic sentence** is a sentence in a paragraph that tells the main idea.
Underline the topic sentence in each paragraph.

1.   Learning to play the piano was not always easy for Todd. He did not always feel like practicing. Sometimes he made a lot of mistakes, even when he was trying hard. Some days, Todd would feel too tired to play. When Todd did start to get better, though, he was very proud.

2.   Kim and Kurt spent $10 each for their stamp albums. Kim bought four special stamps from France. They cost $1 each. Kurt spent $6 on a set of Olympic stamps. Collecting stamps was going to be expensive for the children!

3.   Winters can be very hard in Vermont. There are often heavy snowfalls with high winds. It can be days before some back roads are plowed. Many people in Vermont chop their own wood. That's very hard work. Many people drive special cars and trucks to get around on the snowy roads.

Adding Fractions

Add. Write each answer in simplest form. The first one has been done for you.

A. $\dfrac{2}{5} + \dfrac{1}{5} = \boxed{\dfrac{3}{5}}$

B. $\dfrac{3}{5} + \dfrac{1}{5} = \boxed{}$

C. $\dfrac{7}{9} + \dfrac{1}{9} = \boxed{}$

D. $\dfrac{1}{5} + \dfrac{2}{5} = \boxed{}$

E. $\dfrac{3}{8} + \dfrac{4}{8} = \boxed{}$

F. $\dfrac{5}{7} + \dfrac{1}{7} = \boxed{}$

F. $\dfrac{1}{4} + \dfrac{3}{4} = \boxed{}$

G. $\dfrac{5}{6} + \dfrac{2}{6} = \boxed{}$

Fraction Addition

Add. Write each answer in simplest form. The first one has been done for you.

A.
$$\frac{1}{6} + \frac{1}{6} = \boxed{\frac{1}{3}}$$

B.
$$\frac{3}{10} + \frac{1}{10} = \boxed{}$$

C.
$$\frac{1}{7} + \frac{3}{7} = \boxed{}$$

D.
$$\frac{6}{7} + \frac{3}{7} = \boxed{}$$

E.
$$\frac{1}{8} + \frac{3}{8} = \boxed{}$$

F.
$$\frac{2}{9} + \frac{5}{9} = \boxed{}$$

G.
$$\frac{5}{9} + \frac{1}{9} = \boxed{}$$

H.
$$\frac{2}{5} + \frac{3}{5} = \boxed{}$$

Adjectives

Find and underline the **adjectives** in each paragraph.

1.   Anna went to the big shoe store with her mother. Anna needed some new shoes. She saw black, shiny shoes and white, ruffled shoes. Anna especially liked the fancy red dress shoes with black and white trim. Anna decided to buy some tan shoes. Anna's mother paid the tall salesman, and Anna wore her new shoes home.

2.   I like to watch the brave firefighters work. They wear large, protective outfits to keep them safe from fire. Firefighters try to save small houses, big houses, and office buildings. They will put out a fire anywhere. Sometimes, I have watched them put out fires in the tall forest behind my neighborhood. I would like to be a brave firefighter when I grow up.

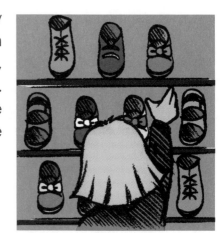

Writing in the Third Person

This story is written from the first person **point of view**. Rewrite the story below, changing the point of view to third person. Add an ending to the story.

A Skating Disaster

I was skating on the sidewalk a few blocks from my house yesterday afternoon when a dog darted out of the bushes. The dog ran right across my path. Boom! Down I fell! I stood up and brushed myself off. Suddenly, a little boy ran out of the same bushes. The boy was calling, "Come back, Pixie!" As he rushed past me, I fell down again. I had just picked myself up again when a man raced out of the bushes! He was shouting, "Come back, Sergio! Come back, Pixie!" I . . .

_____

_____

_____

_____

_____

_____

_____

_____

_____

_____

_____

_____

Analogies

Compare the relationships of the words below.
Write a word on the line to complete each analogy.

1. car : driver : : plane : _____

2. bird : sky : : fish : _____

3. coffee : drink : : hamburger : _____

4. small : tiny : : large : _____

5. glove : hand : : boot : _____

6. easy : simple : : hard : _____

7. breakfast : lunch : : morning : _____

8. blue : color : : round : _____

9. date : calendar : : time : _____

10. win : lose : : stop : _____

Subtracting Fractions

Math

Subtract. Write each answer in simplest form. The first one has been done for you.

A.
$$\frac{2}{3} - \frac{1}{3} = \boxed{\frac{1}{3}}$$

B.
$$\frac{7}{9} - \frac{5}{9} = \boxed{}$$

C.
$$\frac{3}{7} - \frac{1}{7} = \boxed{}$$

D.
$$\frac{3}{5} - \frac{1}{5} = \boxed{}$$

E.
$$\frac{5}{8} - \frac{2}{8} = \boxed{}$$

F.
$$\frac{3}{4} - \frac{1}{4} = \boxed{}$$

G.
$$\frac{8}{9} - \frac{3}{9} = \boxed{}$$

H.
$$\frac{4}{6} - \frac{2}{6} = \boxed{}$$

Mixed Problem Puzzle

Solve the problems. Use the number key at the bottom
of the page to color the picture.

2 + 8 =

2 x 5 =

12 + 4 =

$4\overline{)48}$

12 − 2 =

8 x 2 =

9 + 3 =

4 x 4 =

$3\overline{)30}$

18 − 2 =

20 − 8 =

18 − 3 =

$\begin{array}{r} 3 \\ \times 4 \end{array}$

5 x 2 =

$2\overline{)30}$

Balloons
50¢

5 + 5 =

10 = yellow   16 = orange
15 = green   12 = purple

Completing Analogies

Fill in the blanks to complete the **analogies**.

1. **Ice** is to **cold** as **steam** is to _____.

2. The **sun** is to **daytime** as the **moon** is to _____.

3. **Perspiration** is to **heat** as **shivering** is to _____.

4. **Birds** are to **flying** as **dolphins** are to _____.

5. **Books** are to **reading** as **radios** are to _____.

6. **Shoes** are to **feet** as **gloves** are to _____.

Subtracting Fractions

Subtract the fractions. Write each answer in simplest form.

A. $\dfrac{6}{7}$ $-\dfrac{2}{7}$

B. $\dfrac{6}{9}$ $-\dfrac{3}{9}$

C. $\dfrac{9}{10}$ $-\dfrac{5}{10}$

D. $\dfrac{5}{8}$ $-\dfrac{2}{8}$

E. $\dfrac{3}{4}$ $-\dfrac{1}{4}$

F. $\dfrac{2}{5}$ $-\dfrac{1}{5}$

G. $\dfrac{8}{9}$ $-\dfrac{1}{9}$

H. $\dfrac{2}{3}$ $-\dfrac{1}{3}$

Writing in the First Person

This story is written from the third person **point of view**. Rewrite the story, changing the point of view to first person. Add an ending to the story.

Soccer Hero

Joey has been playing soccer for three years. His team is called the Mountain Lions. Joey plays goalie on the team. A goalie tries to keep the other team from scoring by standing in front of the net and blocking any balls kicked toward it. Joey is a great goalie. He played on the All-Star Team last year. Last Thursday, the Mountain Lions played a team called the Blazing Suns. The Suns were ahead by two goals. The game was almost over and it looked like the Lions were going to lose. Joey . . .

_____

_____

_____

_____

_____

_____

_____

_____

_____

_____

_____

Proofreading

Circle each letter that should be capitalized.
Add punctuation marks in the proper places.
Write an ending to the story.

Creature from Outer Space

tim and i decided to camp out in the backyard we got our sleeping bags two flashlights and some snacks we unrolled our sleeping bags lay down and began to munch on some pretzels it was a clear night and the stars were sparkling brightly tim found the big dipper and the north star one bright star seemed to be moving we watched it race across the sky suddenly it stopped and began to grow bigger it was coming toward us it came to a stop right over our heads now we could see that it was not a star at all it was a spaceship a beam of light shot from the spaceship and glowed all around tim . . .

_____

_____

_____

_____

_____

_____

_____

Tic-Tac-Toe Synonyms

In each tic-tac-toe grid, circle three words in a row that are **synonyms**.

1.

big	above	over
love	large	below
old	hate	giant

2.

front	awful	baby
back	terrible	good
start	horrible	lovely

3.

cry	whisper	sing
weep	spell	come
sob	silly	rise

4.

wet	hot	cold
near	icy	warm
chilly	rain	far

Math

Adding & Subtracting Fractions

Add or **subtract** the mixed numbers. Write each answer in simplest form.

A. $3\frac{3}{5}$
   $+\ 5\frac{1}{5}$
   _____

B. $2\frac{2}{3}$
   $-\ 1\frac{1}{3}$
   _____

C. $8\frac{9}{11}$
   $-\ 4\frac{5}{11}$
   _____

D. $6\frac{3}{4}$
   $-\ 2\frac{1}{4}$
   _____

E. $4\frac{4}{8}$
   $+\ 3\frac{2}{8}$
   _____

F. $9\frac{2}{6}$
   $+\ 1\frac{2}{6}$
   _____

Antonym Puzzle

Color the areas green that contain pairs of antonyms.
Color the rest of the design yellow.

empty
full

pretty
ugly

hot
cold

g
h

early
late

run
away

smile
frown

short
long

fat
thin

noisy
quiet

paper
clip

blue
aqua

dirty
clean

dull
sharp

Measure Sense

Using the chart, circle the measurement choice that is most reasonable.

STANDARD LENGTH
12 in. = 1 ft. **Inch (in.):** the diameter of a quarter
3 ft. = 1 yd. **Foot (ft.):** from your shoulder to elbow
5,280 ft. = 1 mi. **Yard (yd.):** length of a teacher's desk
Mile (mi.): a short car ride

A. length of a fooball field	**B.** width of a math book	**C.** height of a fence	**D.** height of a desk
100 yd. 100 mi.	8 in. 8 ft.	4 in. 4 ft.	2 in. 2 ft.
E. height of a doorway	**F.** width of your wrist	**G.** length of a parking lot	**H.** length of your foot
7 in. 7 ft.	3 in. 3 ft.	50 yd. 50 mi.	7 in. 7 ft.

Conversion Excursion

Use the conversion chart to complete the statements below.

Standard Length

12 in.	=	1 ft.
3 ft.	=	1 yd.
5,280 ft.	=	1 mi.
1,760 yd.	=	1 mi.

24 in. = _____ ft.   6 yd. = _____ ft.   12 ft. = _____ yd.

10,560 ft. = _____ mi.   36 in. = _____ ft.   60 in. = _____ ft.

48 in. = _____ ft.   1 yd. = _____ in.   5 yd. = _____ ft.

36 ft. = _____ yd.   1 ft. = _____ in.   10 ft. = _____ in.

Flying Disc Science

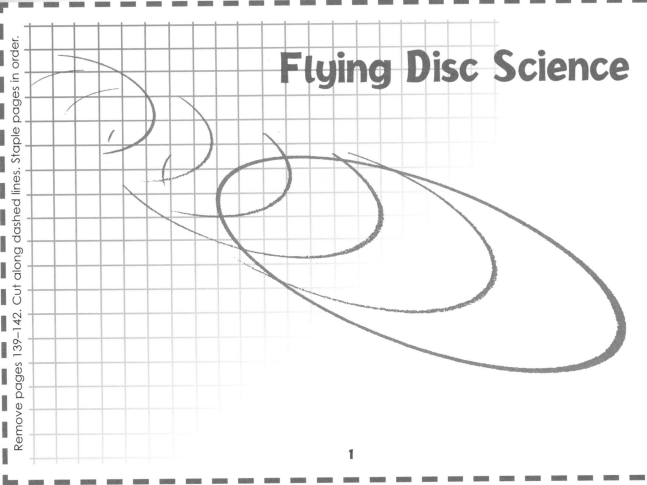

1

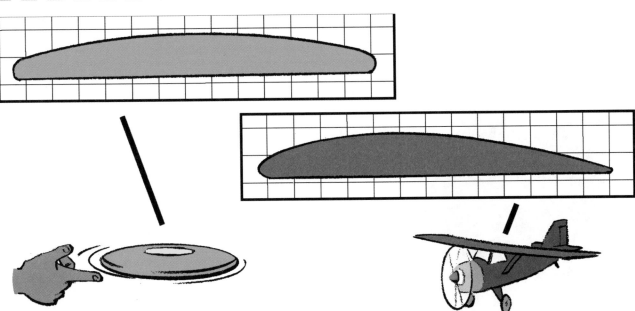

Have you ever wondered what makes a flying disc fly? How is it that an object with such a simple shape can travel through the air for so far and for so long? After all, it's just a lightweight plastic disc.

But look closer. You will notice that the sides are rounded and the top of it is raised. Some of the same ideas behind the design of a flying disc can be found in a sketch of an airplane wing. Don't worry—you won't need a pilot's license to throw a flying disc. But it won't hurt to know why the designs of both objects are similar.

3

Did you know that more flying discs are sold each year than footballs, baseballs, and basketballs combined? How is it that a simple round disc could bring so much fun to so many people?

Perhaps it's because the flying disc isn't as simple as it may seem. Even its history is complicated. The original design came from pie tins made by the Frisbie Baking Company in 1871. These tins started to turn up on college campuses, but not just because they contained delicious pies. The students, after enjoying a tasty dessert, discovered that if you tossed a tin in just the right way, with a sharp twist of the wrist, the tin could soar for many yards. It became a fun, new toy.

Then, in 1948, Walter Morrison and Warren Franscioni decided to make a plastic version of the Frisbie pie tin. They called the toy the Pluto Platter because the disc looked like a UFO. When the toy company Wham-O purchased the invention, they renamed it the Frisbee®. Ten years later, "Frisbee®" was a household word in the United States.

2

A flying disc throw is really a contest of forces. A **force** pushes or pulls an object in some direction. Some forces try to keep the Frisbee moving through the air. Others try to bring it to a stop.

The first force that acts on a flying disc is called **thrust**. Thrust is a force that pushes on an object. When you throw a flying disc, you're pushing it through the air. A jet engine does the same thing to an airplane. It pushes the plane into the air and keeps it there.

So without thrust, the plastic disc wouldn't move at all. There's not much point in having a flying disc if you're just going to let it sit there.

4

The thrust applied to a flying disc is opposed by another force called **air resistance**. It pushes back against the flying disc, reducing the amount of thrust. Have you ever gone for a bike ride and noticed the air beating against your face and messing up your hair? The same thing happens to the plastic disc. Air pushes against it, slowing the disc down as it flies through it.

This is one of the reasons why the edges of the plastic disc are round. The air rolls over the flying disc a lot easier this way than if the edges were straight up and down. The same is true for the airplane wing. See how the front of it is smooth and curved? This shape makes it easier for the plane to slide through the air.

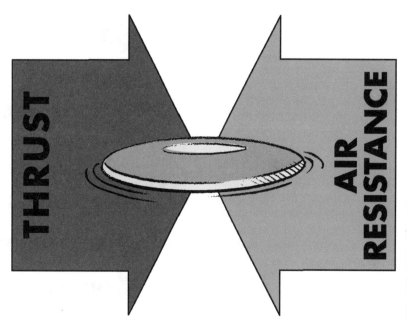

5

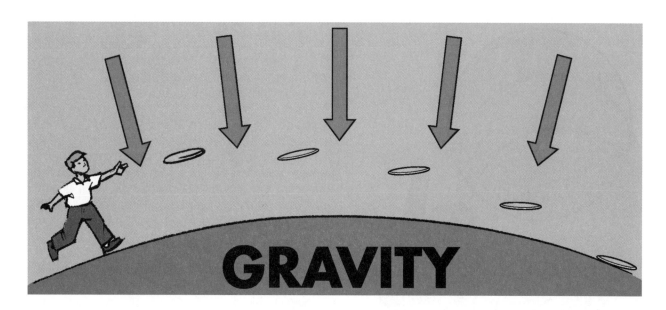

So why doesn't the flying disc just float off into space since air is constantly pushing it upwards? It's because the force of **gravity** is pulling down on the plastic disc, too. Earth's gravity pulls all the objects on its surface toward its center. That's why we don't float off into space.

If no one catches a tossed plastic disc, eventually gravity will win and the flying disc will land on the ground. If there were no such thing as gravity, you could throw a flying disc for a very long way.

7

The flying disc's curved sides and top cause another force to help its flight. This force is called **lift**. Just as it sounds, this force lifts an object into the air and lets it soar.

Because of the disc's rounded sides, air passing across the top of it has a longer distance to travel than it does along its flat bottom. To catch up with the air moving below it, the air on top has to move faster. When the air speeds up, it has less time to push down on the flying disc's top. The slower air beneath the flat bottom of the disc has more time to push up on it. And so, the air lifts the plastic disc.

The same thing happens to an airplane wing. The air beneath the wing pushes up on it, keeping the plane in the air. Without lift, air travel would not be possible.

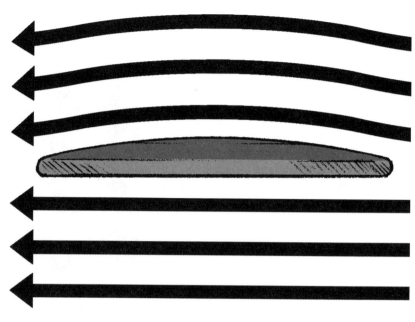

6

Have you ever had trouble throwing a flying disc straight? The reason for this is that you might not be putting enough spin on it. In order to throw a flying disc, you have to snap your wrist. This causes the plastic disc to spin rapidly as it flies through the air. Much like a toy top, the spinning keeps the disc from wobbling and flying in all kinds of crazy directions. If you don't snap your wrist when you toss it, your flying disc will probably crash to the ground soon after you let it go. That's not much fun for the person waiting to catch it.

It is also important to hold the disc level when you toss it. If you don't, you'll see your flying disc curving away from the friend you've tossed it to. Try keeping the disc level and see how that works.

Of course, throwing a flying disc isn't as simple as it looks, but once you learn how to do it, your next trip to the beach or park will be a lot more fun!

8

Spelling Assessment

Read each group of words. Mark the word that is **not** spelled correctly.

1. ☐ several
   ☐ skirt
   ☐ spiret
   ☐ strain
   ☐ torn

2. ☐ yawn
   ☐ yourselves
   ☐ wow
   ☐ wastte
   ☐ twin

3. ☐ tomato
   ☐ sword
   ☐ stole
   ☐ sparkel
   ☐ sixth

4. ☐ serve
   ☐ ruber
   ☐ rear
   ☐ prepare
   ☐ pinch

5. ☐ pad
   ☐ neklace
   ☐ mess
   ☐ knife
   ☐ hero

6. ☐ footprint
   ☐ fern
   ☐ dozzen
   ☐ degree
   ☐ create

7. ☐ coast
   ☐ cellar
   ☐ broom
   ☐ behav
   ☐ attention

8. ☐ gloom
   ☐ footstep
   ☐ envelope
   ☐ drag
   ☐ creeture

9. ☐ cent
   ☐ belly
   ☐ attick
   ☐ address
   ☐ account

10. ☐ avenue
    ☐ bufalo
    ☐ colorful
    ☐ croak
    ☐ dentist

11. ☐ dredful
    ☐ event
    ☐ fifty
    ☐ forward
    ☐ goodbye

12. ☐ guy
    ☐ history
    ☐ ink
    ☐ lace
    ☐ lowwer

13. ☐ pale
    ☐ sadle
    ☐ shady
    ☐ slam
    ☐ stray

14. ☐ tan
    ☐ tough
    ☐ undergroun
    ☐ warmth
    ☐ tin

15. ☐ mist
    ☐ nibble
    ☐ place
    ☐ pitcker
    ☐ princess

16. ☐ rust
    ☐ skunk
    ☐ spit
    ☐ tame
    ☐ yeserday

17. ☐ warn
    ☐ twice
    ☐ tip
    ☐ stirr
    ☐ sip

18. ☐ rowboat
    ☐ readder
    ☐ pill
    ☐ package
    ☐ neat

19. ☐ merry
    ☐ lood
    ☐ herd
    ☐ guide
    ☐ glitter

20. ☐ ache
    ☐ awakken
    ☐ birdhouse
    ☐ buggy
    ☐ charm

21. ☐ comb
    ☐ crocoodile
    ☐ department
    ☐ examine
    ☐ gym

22. ☐ actual
    ☐ acorn
    ☐ aim
    ☐ awerd
    ☐ birth

23. ☐ chatter
    ☐ comfort
    ☐ crooke
    ☐ depend
    ☐ drift

24. ☐ example
    ☐ fought
    ☐ haircut
    ☐ inssist
    ☐ laid

25. ☐ lung
    ☐ mister
    ☐ noble
    ☐ plannet
    ☐ sadness

26. ☐ shagy
    ☐ slant
    ☐ split
    ☐ tangle
    ☐ tour

27. ☐ sort
    ☐ single
    ☐ Septeber
    ☐ ray
    ☐ lizard

28. ☐ helpless
    ☐ geust
    ☐ glide
    ☐ football
    ☐ female

Narrative Passage

Read the story, then read each question. Read all the answers and mark the space for the answer you think is right. Mark NH (not here) if the answer can not be figured out from the given information.

Lillian slid lower in her chair. She was almost under her desk. If she could just disappear, maybe the teacher wouldn't call on her. Lillian was prepared. She loved to read and had finished the book two weeks ago. She also liked to write, so the book report was no problem. Lillian did not want to read her report to the class. Her stomach felt sick and her face got hot every time she thought about standing up in front of all those children. The teacher called Lillian's name. Lillian slowly stood up and shuffled to the front of the room. She thought about Sam, a character in her book. If only she could be as brave as he was. Suddenly, Lillian knew what to do! She closed her eyes and pretended she was Sam. She told Sam's story, just as if it had happened to her. When she was finished, Lillian opened her eyes and looked at the class in front of her. They were clapping wildly because she had given such a good report! The teacher was very happy and gave Lillian an A+ on her report. Lillian was happy, too!

1. Why was Lillian trying to hide under her desk?
   ○ **She did not want to give the report.**
   ○ **She was not feeling well.**
   ○ **She always hid under there.**
   ○ NH

2. Lillian was afraid of something. What was she afraid of?
   ○ **reading aloud**
   ○ **standing up in front of the class**
   ○ **her teacher**
   ○ NH

3. Why did the teacher make Lillian give the report?
   ○ **She didn't like Lillian.**
   ○ **It was Lillian's turn to report.**
   ○ **She wanted Lillian to be brave.**
   ○ NH

4. How did Lillian help herself get through the report?
   ○ **She pretended she was at home.**
   ○ **She pretended to be brave.**
   ○ **She pretended to be Sam.**
   ○ NH

5. What words from the story give clues about how Lillian felt giving book reports in front of the class?
   ○ **brave, pretended, wildly**
   ○ **happy, character, problem**
   ○ **disappear, sick, shuffled**
   ○ NH

6. What grade did Lillian get for her report?
   ○ A+
   ○ E+
   ○ A
   ○ NH

Vocabulary Assessment

Read the first part of the sentence and look at the underlined word or phrase. Choose the word that means about the same thing as the underlined word or phrase. Mark the correct answer.

1. To make something look larger is to . . .
   - ○ shovel
   - ○ lighten
   - ○ magnify

2. To save something is to . . .
   - ○ preserve
   - ○ outwit
   - ○ lasso

3. Something that is strong and solid is . . .
   - ○ hoarse
   - ○ sturdy
   - ○ harmful

4. Something evil or bad is . . .
   - ○ wicked
   - ○ mischief
   - ○ slender

5. To surprise greatly is to . . .
   - ○ astonish
   - ○ cradle
   - ○ involve

6. To sort or put things into categories is to . . .
   - ○ educate
   - ○ insult
   - ○ classify

7. A strong feeling of wanting to know or learn is . . .
   - ○ lark
   - ○ curiosity
   - ○ harmony

8. Something that has no feeling is . . .
   - ○ society
   - ○ mixture
   - ○ numb

9. A smell or odor is a . . .
   - ○ humor
   - ○ dipper
   - ○ scent

10. A person visiting a new place is a . . .
    - ○ twitch
    - ○ runaway
    - ○ tourist

11. To move forward is to . . .
    - ○ advance
    - ○ salute
    - ○ skim

12. Something that has a strong, unpleasant taste is . . .
    - ○ fiery
    - ○ bitter
    - ○ crimson

13. The power to work or be active is . . .
    - ○ energy
    - ○ glimpse
    - ○ display

14. A motion made with the arms is a . . .
    - ○ freckle
    - ○ gesture
    - ○ custodian

15. To move a little is to . . .
    - ○ budge
    - ○ dimple
    - ○ lend

16. To worry is to be . . .
    - ○ concerned
    - ○ lame
    - ○ eerie

17. A strong dislike that makes you feel sick is called . . .
    - ○ length
    - ○ disgust
    - ○ reflection

18. Something very good is . . .
    - ○ shatter
    - ○ modest
    - ○ fantastic

19. A person who tells the truth is . . .
    - ○ hasty
    - ○ honest
    - ○ horrified

20. To want what others have is to be . . .
    - ○ beaten
    - ○ classical
    - ○ jealous

21. A smell is an . . .
    - ○ diagram
    - ○ odor
    - ○ crime

Place Value with Large Numbers

Use the given number to find the place values. The first one has been done for you.

1. The number is: **7,320,194.685**

   a. Name the digit in the tens place. _____ 9 _____

   b. Name the digit in the tenths place. _____

   c. Name the digit in the millions place. _____

   d. Name the digit in the ones place. _____

   e. In what place value is the digit 0? _____

   f. In what place is the digit 2? _____

   g. In what place value is the digit 3? _____

   h. In what place value is the digit 5? _____

2. The number is: **8,635.147**

   a. Name the digit in the hundreds place. _____

   b. Name the digit in the hundredths place. _____

   c. Name the digit in the thousands place. _____

   d. Name the digit in the tenths place. _____

   e. Name the number that is one hundred more. _____

   f. Name the number that is one thousand less. _____

   g. Name the number that is one-hundredth less. _____

   h. Name the number that is one more. _____

3. The number is: **1,320,796.485**

   a. Name the digit in the millions place. _____

   b. Name the digit in the ones place. _____

   c. Name the digit in the thousandths place. _____

   d. Name the digit in the ten thousands place. _____

   e. Name the number that is ten thousand less. _____

   f. Name the number that is one-thousandth more. _____

   g. Name the number that is one less. _____

   h. Name the number that is one million more. _____

Answer Key

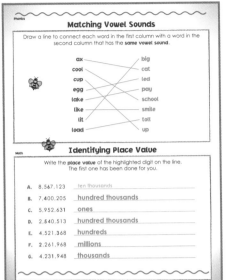

Matching Vowel Sounds
Draw a line to connect each word in the first column with a word in the second column that has the same vowel sound.

ax	big
cool	cat
cup	led
egg	pay
lake	school
like	smile
lit	toll
load	up

Identifying Place Value
Write the place value of the highlighted digit on the line. The first one has been done for you.

A. 8,567,123 — ten thousands
B. 7,400,205 — hundred thousands
C. 5,952,631 — ones
D. 2,540,513 — hundred thousands
E. 4,521,368 — hundreds
F. 2,261,968 — millions
G. 4,231,948 — thousands

16

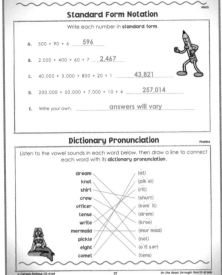

Standard Form Notation
Write each number in standard form.

A. 500 + 90 + 6 — 596
B. 2,000 + 400 + 60 + 7 — 2,467
C. 40,000 + 3,000 + 800 + 20 + 1 — 43,821
D. 200,000 + 50,000 + 7,000 + 10 + 4 — 257,014
E. Write your own. — answers will vary

Dictionary Pronunciation
Listen to the vowel sounds in each word below, then draw a line to connect each word with its dictionary pronunciation.

dream	(at)
knot	(pik'el)
shirt	(rit)
crew	(shurt)
officer	(kom' it)
tense	(drem)
write	(kroo)
mermaid	(mur' mad)
pickle	(not)
eight	(o'fi sər)
comet	(tens)

17

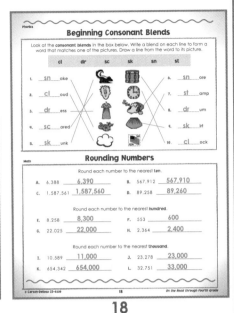

Beginning Consonant Blends
Look at the consonant blends in the box below. Write a blend on each line to form a word that matches one of the pictures. Draw a line from the word to its picture.

cl   dr   sc   sk   sn   st

1. sn ake
2. cl oud
3. dr ess
4. sc ared
5. sk unk
6. sn ore
7. st amp
8. dr um
9. sk irt
10. cl ock

Rounding Numbers
Round each number to the nearest ten.

A. 6,388 — 6,390
B. 567,912 — 567,910
C. 1,587,561 — 1,587,560
D. 89,258 — 89,260

Round each number to the nearest hundred.

E. 8,258 — 8,300
F. 553 — 600
G. 22,025 — 22,000
H. 2,364 — 2,400

Round each number to the nearest thousand.

I. 10,589 — 11,000
J. 23,278 — 23,000
K. 654,342 — 654,000
L. 32,751 — 33,000

18

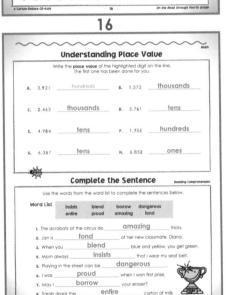

Understanding Place Value
Write the place value of the highlighted digit on the line. The first one has been done for you.

A. 3,921 — hundreds
B. 1,572 — thousands
C. 2,463 — thousands
D. 5,761 — tens
E. 4,984 — tens
F. 1,756 — hundreds
G. 6,357 — tens
H. 6,852 — ones

Complete the Sentence
Use the words from the word list to complete the sentences below.

Word List: insists   blend   borrow   dangerous   entire   proud   amazing   fond

1. The acrobats at the circus do **amazing** tricks.
2. Jan is **fond** of her new classmate, Diana.
3. When you **blend** blue and yellow, you get green.
4. Mom always **insists** that I wear my seat belt.
5. Playing in the street can be **dangerous**.
6. I was **proud** when I won first prize.
7. May I **borrow** your eraser?
8. Sarah drank the **entire** carton of milk.

19

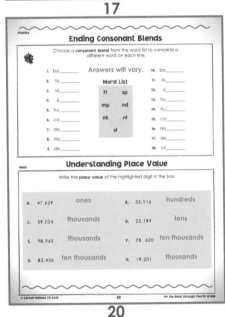

Ending Consonant Blends
Choose a consonant blend from the word list to complete a different word on each line.

Answers will vary.

Word List: ft   sp   mp   nd   nk   nt   st

1. ba___
2. la___
3. si___
4. si___
5. tru___
6. ca___
7. da___
8. de___
9. de___
10. ba___
11. la___
12. tru___
13. tru___
14. tru___
15. ca___
16. de___
17. de___
18. cri___

Understanding Place Value
Write the place value of the highlighted digit in the box.

A. 47,629 — ones
B. 35,116 — hundreds
C. 59,024 — thousands
D. 23,199 — tens
E. 98,965 — thousands
F. 78,620 — ten thousands
G. 83,456 — ten thousands
H. 19,201 — thousands

20

A Friendly Letter
Write a letter to your favorite actor or actress. Include all five parts of a friendly letter. Remember to put a comma after the greeting and closing.

Letters will vary.

Addressing an Envelope
Address the envelope below using the information given.

The sender is:
Mr. Fred Barrow
216 Dawson Drive
Ogden, UT 66065

The receiver is:
Ms. Carla George
22 W. 42nd Street
Tampa, FL 21563

Mr. Fred Barrow
216 Dawson Drive
Ogden, UT 66065

Ms. Carla George
22 W. 42nd Street
Tampa, FL 21563

21

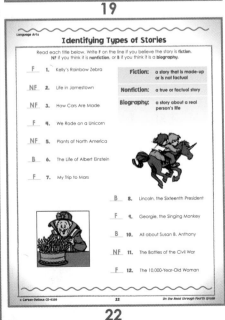

Identifying Types of Stories
Read each title below. Write F on the line if you believe the story is fiction, NF if you think it is nonfiction, or B if you think it is a biography.

Fiction: a story that is made-up or is not factual
Nonfiction: a true or factual story
Biography: a story about a real person's life

F 1. Kelly's Rainbow Zebra
NF 2. Life in Jamestown
NF 3. How Cars Are Made
F 4. We Rode on a Unicorn
NF 5. Plants of North America
B 6. The Life of Albert Einstein
F 7. My Trip to Mars
B 8. Lincoln, the Sixteenth President
F 9. Georgie, the Singing Monkey
B 10. All about Susan B. Anthony
NF 11. The Battles of the Civil War
F 12. The 10,000-Year-Old Woman

22

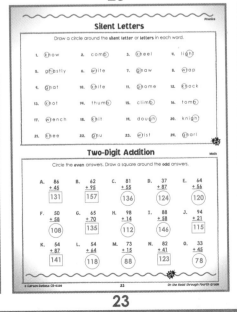

Silent Letters
Draw a circle around the silent letter or letters in each word.

1. know
2. comb
3. kneel
4. light
5. ghastly
6. write
7. gnaw
8. wrap
9. gnat
10. knife
11. gnome
12. knock
13. knot
14. thumb
15. climb
16. tomb
17. wrench
18. knit
19. dough
20. knight
21. knee
22. why
23. wrist
24. gnarl

Two-Digit Addition
Circle the even answers. Draw a square around the odd answers.

A. 86 + 45 = 131
B. 62 + 95 = 157
C. 81 + 55 = 136
D. 37 + 87 = 124
E. 64 + 56 = 120
F. 50 + 58 = 108
G. 65 + 70 = 135
H. 98 + 14 = 112
I. 88 + 58 = 146
J. 94 + 21 = 115
K. 54 + 87 = 141
L. 54 + 64 = 118
M. 73 + 15 = 88
N. 82 + 41 = 123
O. 33 + 45 = 78

23

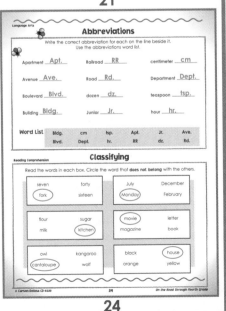

Abbreviations
Write the correct abbreviation for each on the line beside it. Use the abbreviations word list.

Apartment — Apt.
Railroad — RR
centimeter — cm
Avenue — Ave.
Road — Rd.
Department — Dept.
Boulevard — Blvd.
dozen — dz.
teaspoon — tsp.
Building — Bldg.
Junior — Jr.
hour — hr.

Word List: Bldg.   cm   tsp.   Apt.   Jr.   Ave.   Blvd.   Dept.   hr.   RR   dz.   Rd.

Classifying
Read the words in each box. Circle the word that does not belong with the others.

seven	forty
fork	sixteen

July	December
Monday	February

flour	sugar
milk	**kitchen**

movie	letter
magazine	book

owl	kangaroo
cantaloupe	wolf

black	**house**
orange	yellow

24

Answer Key

Following Directions

Follow the directions to draw a picture in the box.

1. Draw a tree with four branches and orange and red leaves in the bottom left corner.
2. Draw a yellow half moon in the upper right corner.
3. Draw a brown fence across the bottom.
4. Draw four gray cats on the fence.
5. Draw six dark clouds in the sky.
6. Draw one owl on a branch of the tree.
7. Draw five black birds flying in the sky.
8. Add any other details you wish.

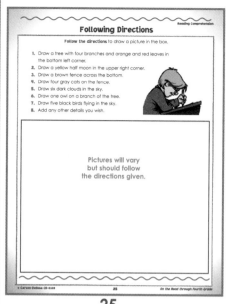

Pictures will vary
but should follow
the directions given.

25

Break the Code

Find the sums. Write the letter next to each problem on the correct lines below to read the coded message.

96 + 58	56 + 86	79 + 38	86 + 27	38 + 85	64 + 83
(T) 154	(V) 142	(D) 117	(E) 113	(K) 125	(D) 147

89 + 47	58 + 62	73 + 49	86 + 76	69 + 52	77 + 54
(U) 136	(G) 120	(A) 122	(V) 162	(H) 121	(R) 131

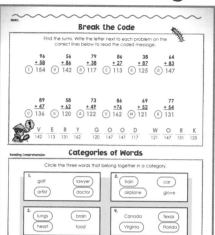

V E R Y   G O O D   W O R K
142 113 131 162   120 120 117   121 147 131 125

Categories of Words

Circle the three words that belong together in a category.

1. (golf) (lawyer) (artist) (doctor)
2. (train) car (airplane) glove
3. (lungs) (brain) (heart) food
4. Canada (Texas) (Virginia) (Florida)
5. (necklace) (ring) balloon (bracelet)
6. (happy) grumpy (embarrassed) (laughter)

26

Alphabetical Order

Write numbers in front of the words in each group to put them in **alphabetical order**.

A.
- 6 king
- 2 keen
- 4 kernel
- 7 knee
- 3 keep
- 5 kind
- 1 kangaroo

B.
- 1 toast
- 2 toffee
- 4 told
- 5 tomorrow
- 6 total
- 3 together
- 7 tough

C.
- 1 egg
- 3 elephant
- 6 ensemble
- 4 elf
- 2 electric
- 5 ending
- 7 especially

Using Math Symbols <, >, or =

Solve each problem. Print the answer next to the correct letter at the bottom.
Place the correct symbol (<, >, or =) in the circle.

A. 22 + 35 = 57 B. 60 + 39 = 99 C. 50 + 31 = 81
D. 63 + 20 = 83 E. 10 + 3 = 13 F. 50 + 25 = 75
G. 77 + 7 = 84 H. 60 + 21 = 81 I. 12 + 30 = 42

57 (<) 84
(A)   (G)

81 (=) 81
(C)   (H)

99 (>) 42
(B)   (I)

75 (>) 13
(F)   (E)

83 (<) 84
(D)   (A)

57 (<) 84
(A)   (G)

27

Cloze

Read the story below. Many words are missing.
Fill in the blanks with words from the word list.

Randy loved to paint. He liked to paint with his fingers **when** he was little. He would paint on **paper**. He would paint on tables. Once he **even** painted on the living room wall! Randy's **parents** were not happy with his painting. They **begged** him to play ball or ride his **bicycle**, but Randy only wanted to paint. When **Randy** was older, he helped the neighbors paint **their** house. He painted a huge but beautiful **flower** on the front of their house. The **neighbors** did not want a huge, beautiful flower **painted** on the front of their house. Randy **lost** that job! Today Randy is very happy. **He** is a famous painter. Now his parents **love** his painting. And the neighbors wish they still had the flower on the front of their house.

Word List
begged
bicycle
even
flower
He
lost
love
painted
paper
parents
Randy
their
when

Three-Digit Addition

Add to solve each problem.

A. 486 + 514 = 1,000	B. 237 + 185 = 422	C. 902 + 404 = 1,306	D. 375 + 612 = 987

E. 842 + 254 = 1,096	F. 951 + 726 = 1,677	G. 33 + 76 + 54 = 163	H. 45 + 48 + 85 = 178

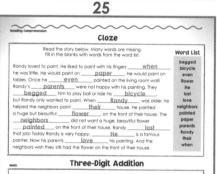

28

Addition with Decimals

Add to solve each problem.

A. 3.5 + 8.2 = 11.7	B. 7.9 + 3.1 = 11.0	C. 9.0 + 4.8 = 13.8	D. 49.5 + 52.4 = 101.9

E. 7.03 + 7.85 = 14.88	F. 3.25 + 4.94 = 8.19	G. 8.03 + 5.13 = 13.16	H. 49.6 + 31.2 = 80.8

Syllables

Read the animal names below. Count the number
of **syllables** in each name. Print the number of syllables in the box.

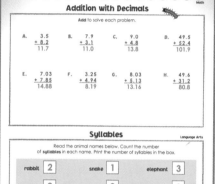

rabbit	2	snake	1	elephant	3
monkey	2	lion	2	giraffe	2
flamingo	3	manatee	3	dinosaur	3
koala	3	wolverine	3	dolphin	2
whale	1	aardvark	2	emu	2

29

Writing Paragraphs

Read the title and main idea of the paragraph. Write your own details.

Title of paragraph: My Best Friend

Main Idea: My best friend is someone special.

Details:
1.
2.
3.
4.

Answers will vary.

Retell the Main Idea: I am glad I have such a great friend.

Use the information above to write a paragraph. Include the main idea and details, then retell the main idea. Indent the first sentence. Use capital letters and periods. Remember to title the paragraph.

Answers will vary.

30

Days of the Week Abbreviations

Write the **abbreviation** for each day of the week.
Then find each word in the word search below.

1. Sunday — Sun.
2. Friday — Fri.
3. Thursday — Thurs.
4. Saturday — Sat.
5. Monday — Mon.
6. Wednesday — Wed.
7. Tuesday — Tues.

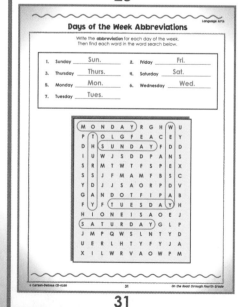

```
M O N D A Y R G H W U
P T O L G F E A C E Y
D H S U N D A Y F D
I U W J S D U N I E X
S R M T W T F S P E V
S J F M A M F B S C
Y D J J S A O R P D V
G A N D O T F I P A B
F Y T U E S D A Y Y
H I O N E I S A O E J
S A T U R D A Y G L P
J M P Q W S L N T Y D
U E R L H T Y F Y J A
X I L W R V A O W P M
```

31

Context Clues

One word has been highlighted in each sentence below. There are two definitions given for the word. Decide which meaning is correct by reading the sentence and thinking about how the word is used. Circle the correct meaning.

1. The **bail** was broken, so the bucket of water was difficult to lift.
   a. throw water out   **b. the handle of a pail**
2. The princess had a grand time at the **ball** last night.
   a. a dance   b. a round object
3. Joe **left** before I could tell him good-bye.
   a. the opposite of right   **b. went away**
4. Jack had a **fit** when his brother broke his new bicycle.
   a. suitable   b. an attack
5. The group became **grave** when they saw the danger they were in.
   a. serious   b. a place of burial

Three-Digit Addition

Time yourself. How fast can you complete the problems?

A. 410 + 291 = 701	737 + 288 = 1,015	426 + 497 = 923	166 + 617 = 783	404 + 395 = 799	259 + 450 = 709	272 + 438 = 710

B. 357 + 417 = 774	519 + 170 = 689	834 + 196 = 1,030	313 + 488 = 801	558 + 184 = 742	687 + 139 = 826	901 + 149 = 1,050

Time: _____   **Number correct:** _____

32

Reading a Bar Graph

The bar graph below shows how many boxes of cookies were sold at Discovery Elementary School over an eight-week period. Use the graph to answer the questions.

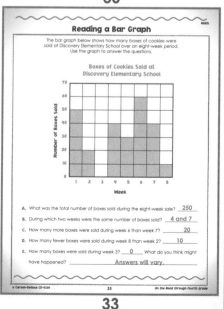

Boxes of Cookies Sold at Discovery Elementary School

(Number of Boxes Sold vs. Week)

A. What was the total number of boxes sold during the eight-week sale? **250**
B. During which two weeks were the same number of boxes sold? **4 and 7**
C. How many more boxes were sold during week 6 than week 7? **20**
D. How many fewer boxes were sold during week 8 than week 2? **10**
E. How many boxes were sold during week 3? **0** What do you think might have happened? **Answers will vary.**

33

Answer Key

Page 34

Math

Three-Digit Column Addition

Add to solve each problem.

A. 402 / 715 / + 513 = 1,630
B. 800 / 240 / + 912 = 1,952
C. 257 / 946 / + 178 = 1,381
D. 589 / 456 / + 981 = 2,026

E. 643 / 285 / 133 / + 341 = 1,402
F. 321 / 419 / 444 / + 750 = 1,934
G. 814 / 901 / 121 / + 215 = 2,051
H. 136 / 912 / 978 / + 222 = 2,248

Reading Comprehension

Riddles

Twenty white horses up a red hill.
Now they chomp. Now they stomp.
Now they stand still.
What are they?

The words in the box make a riddle. They have a hidden meaning. Can you guess what the riddle is about? The answer is teeth! There are twenty white teeth in your mouth. The red hill is your gums. As you talk, they move up and down as if they are chomping and stomping. When you finish talking, they "stand still."

Riddles give a symbolic meaning to things. They have been used for thousands of years. In ancient times, wise people would often answer questions with riddles. It was believed that knowledge was precious, or of great value, and should not be given to everyone. If a person could solve a riddle, he was smart enough to know the answer.

1. What is the main idea of this story?
   a. Riddles are used as symbols.
   b. Riddles have been used for many years.
   c. Riddles are hard to figure out.

2. What is a riddle? __Words that give symbolic meaning to something__

3. The word **precious** means:
   a. a lot of money
   b. meaning
   c. **valuable**

4. Instead of giving an answer, why did wise people speak in riddles? __Only smart or wise people could figure out the answers.__

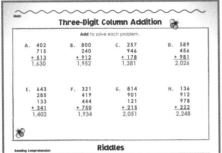

© Carson-Dellosa CD-0320 — 34 — *On the Road through Fourth Grade*

Page 35

Language Arts

Alphabetical Order

Write the months in **alphabetical order** on the lines. Then, write the **abbreviation** beside each month. Circle the month of your birthday.

Word List

January	February	March	April	September	June
December	August	May	October	November	July

1. April — Apr.
2. August — Aug.
3. December — Dec.
4. February — Feb.
5. January — Jan.
6. July
7. June
8. March — Mar.
9. May
10. November — Nov.
11. October — Oct.
12. September — Sept.

Word Problems

Solve each word problem.

A. Dexter made $5.00 washing cars on Monday, $2.75 on Tuesday, and $6.25 on Wednesday. How much money did Dexter make in the three days of car washing?

__$14.00__

B. Missy took 114 pictures last June, 121 last July, and 109 last August. How many pictures did Missy take last summer?

__344 pictures__

C. Kerry ate two oranges at breakfast and half an orange at lunch. At dinner, Kerry ate the other half of the orange from lunch. How many oranges did Kerry eat?

__3 oranges__

D. Sandy sold 65 books at the book sale on Thursday, 231 books on Friday, and 111 more on Saturday. How many books did Sandy sell in three days?

__407 books__

© Carson-Dellosa CD-0320 — 35 — *On the Road through Fourth Grade*

Page 36

Math

Three-Digit Addition

Add to solve problems.

A. 358 / + 227 = 585
B. 371 / + 389 = 760
C. 408 / + 159 = 567
D. 327 / + 196 = 523
E. 730 / + 197 = 927
F. 344 / + 523 = 867

G. 751 / + 225 = 976
H. 400 / + 127 = 527
I. 111 / + 345 = 456
J. 250 / + 178 = 428
K. 382 / + 160 = 542
L. 348 / + 436 = 784

M. 428 / + 150 = 578
N. 197 / + 402 = 599
O. 724 / + 150 = 874
P. 181 / + 199 = 380
Q. 451 / + 315 = 766
R. 613 / + 178 = 791

Reading Comprehension

Cloze

Read the story below. Many words are missing. Fill in the blanks with the from the word list.

Word List: danced, down, had, peeking, puddles, pulled, reached, red, stepped, Sure, was, weather, would

Hunting for a Rainbow

Maggie pulled the rubber boots on over her shoes. She slid into her yellow raincoat and __pulled__ the front closed. This was just the __weather__ she had been hoping for. The sky __was__ a light gray with bits of blue __peeking__ through. Maggie knew that this time she __would__ find what she was looking for. She __stepped__ outside and opened the big __red__ umbrella over her head. The light rain __danced__ on the rounded top and quickly slid __down__ the sides. Her boots splashed in the __puddles__ as Maggie walked through them. The rain __had__ almost stopped so Maggie hurried faster. She __reached__ the top of the hill and looked. __Sure__ enough, this time she found it! Beyond the hill was a beautiful rainbow sparkling in the sun.

© Carson-Dellosa CD-0320 — 36 — *On the Road through Fourth Grade*

Page 41

Language Arts

Antonym Search

Match each pair of antonyms by connecting a word from the first column of the word list with a word from the second column. Then, find and circle each antonym pair in the word search. (Hint: Each pair of words is spelled across and down and shares one letter.) One pair has already been done for you.

Word List

left	little
big	right
small	late
early	close
open	large
fresh	go
stop	long
short	stale
hot	bottom
noisy	quiet
top	cold

© Carson-Dellosa CD-0320 — 41 — *On the Road through Fourth Grade*

Page 42

Language Arts

Can You Spell?

Underline the **spelling error** in each sentence. Write the **correct spelling** of the word on the line.

1. Are you goeing to the ball game? — going
2. My room is very cleen. — clean
3. Ronnie baught some gum at the store. — bought
4. Tony payed $15.00 to get his bike fixed. — paid
5. Pepper makes Becky sneaze. — sneeze
6. Billy loves ice creem. — cream
7. Travis is very frendly. — friendly

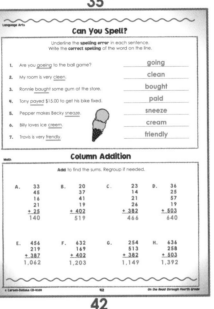

Math

Column Addition

Add to find the sums. Regroup if needed.

A. 33 / 45 / 16 / 21 / + 25 = 140
B. 20 / 37 / 41 / 19 / + 402 = 519
C. 23 / 14 / 21 / 26 / + 382 = 466
D. 36 / 25 / 57 / 19 / + 503 = 640

E. 456 / 219 / + 387 = 1,062
F. 632 / 169 / + 402 = 1,203
G. 254 / 513 / + 382 = 1,149
H. 636 / 258 / + 503 = 1,392

© Carson-Dellosa CD-0320 — 42 — *On the Road through Fourth Grade*

Page 43

Language Arts

Alphabetical Order

Write the words from the word list in **alphabetical order** on the lines.

1. asteroid
2. astronauts
3. Earth
4. Jupiter
5. Mars
6. Mercury
7. moon
8. Neptune
9. planet
10. Pluto
11. satellite
12. Saturn
13. shuttle
14. universe
15. Uranus
16. Venus

Word List

Mars	Venus
Mercury	Jupiter
Uranus	Neptune
satellite	universe
planet	shuttle
Earth	asteroid
Saturn	Pluto
moon	astronauts

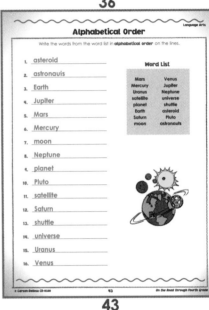

© Carson-Dellosa CD-0320 — 43 — *On the Road through Fourth Grade*

Page 44

Grammar

Types of Sentences

Read each sentence. Using the key, write the corresponding letter on the line to name the sentence type. Then, write the correct **punctuation** at the end of the sentence.

S 1. Carol lives in a pretty house .
Q 2. Does Joyce like peanut butter ?
S 3. We miss Terry very much .
C 4. Take Timmy's cat to his house .
E 5. Wow, Kenneth hit a home run !
E 6. Ouch, that hurt !

Key
C = Command
E = Exclamation
S = Statement
Q = Question

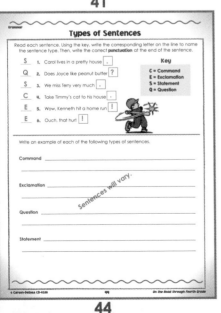

Write an example of each of the following types of sentences.

Command _____

Sentences will vary.

Exclamation _____

Question _____

Statement _____

© Carson-Dellosa CD-0320 — 44 — *On the Road through Fourth Grade*

Page 45

Language Arts

Compound Words

Write a word from the word list on each line to form a **compound word**. Find each compound word in the word search at the bottom of the page.

Word List: work, brush, noon, foot, ball, board, burger, stick, fall, corn, mark, bell

after __noon__
bare __foot__
book __mark__
cheese __burger__
water __fall__
pop __corn__
tooth __brush__
skate __board__
candle __stick__
base __ball__
home __work__
door __bell__

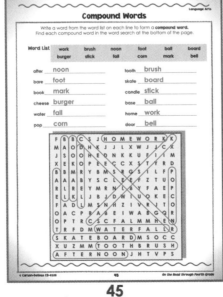

© Carson-Dellosa CD-0320 — 45 — *On the Road through Fourth Grade*

Page 46

Reading Comprehension

Building Vocabulary

Beth wants to be a paramedic and she practices on her dog, Gumbo. Read the story to see how Gumbo feels about all of this. Then, read each of the five sentences. Write the letter for the best answer on the line.

Good Old Gumbo . . .

No dog was ever as patient as Gumbo. Just ask Beth. She is his owner. Beth has put Gumbo through a great deal in his young life. He's been a model for **assorted** doll clothes. He's **retrieved** baseballs from under thick hedges. Now Gumbo is a model again. This time it's for splints and bandages.

Beth's learning all about first aid. She hopes to be a paramedic one day. She thinks helping people would be a good thing. She wants to practice every bandage and splint on Gumbo.

After only five minutes, Gumbo has become **disturbed**. He doesn't think being wrapped up is much fun. He decides that he'd better do something **immediately**. He has heard the saying, "being all tied up." Gumbo wants to get out of this while he still can!

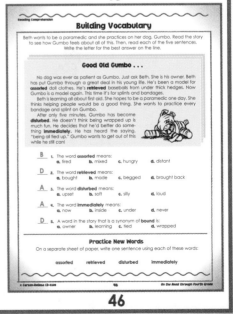

1. The word **assorted** means: — B
   a. tired   b. mixed   c. hungry   d. distant

2. The word **retrieved** means: — D
   a. bought   b. made   c. begged   d. brought back

3. The word **disturbed** means: — A
   a. upset   b. soft   c. silly   d. loud

4. The word **immediately** means: — A
   a. now   b. inside   c. under   d. never

5. A word in the story that is a synonym of **bound** is: — D
   a. owner   b. learning   c. tied   d. wrapped

Practice New Words

On a separate sheet of paper, write one sentence using each of these words.

assorted   retrieved   disturbed   immediately

© Carson-Dellosa CD-0320 — 46 — *On the Road through Fourth Grade*

Answer Key

Main Idea

The **main idea** of a paragraph is its central thought or topic. Read each paragraph. Read the three phrases under each paragraph. Decide which one tells the main idea. Write the letter of that phrase on the line.

B 1. Gary and Fritz have been writing to each other for four years. Gary lives in Indiana and Fritz lives in Germany. Gary looks forward to Fritz's letters. Fritz usually sends at least one picture and sometimes he sends extra German stamps for Gary's collection. Gary and Fritz both hope that they can meet someday. They feel as if they know each other already.

    a. Pictures from Germany   **b.** Gary's German pen pal   **c.** Gary's friend

C 2. Mary has been blind all of her life. She has gone to special schools to learn to do things for herself. Her best friend Katy is not blind. Katy and Mary help each other. Mary is trying to teach Katy to read Braille. It is a special system of raised dots that lets Mary "read" the page. Katy isn't doing very well at all. Katy says that it is hard for her to "see" the letters with her fingers.

    a. Learning to read   **b.** Understanding Braille   **c.** A special friendship

What's Missing?

Print the correct number in the box to complete each number sentence.

A. 2 + **11** = 13   B. 38 − **14** = 24   C. 28 − **13** = 15

D. 73 + **16** = 89   E. 40 − **7** = 33   F. 82 + **15** = 97

G. 55 + **18** = 73   H. 56 − **43** = 13   I. 19 + **14** = 33

J. 26 + **9** = 35   K. 28 − **9** = 19   L. 77 − **18** = 59

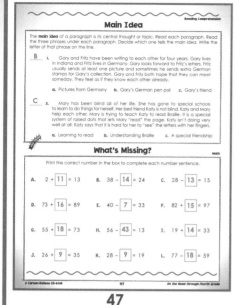

47

Two-Digit Subtraction Review

Calculate the following **subtraction** problems. Regroup as needed.

A. 15 − 5 = 10	B. 25 − 3 = 22	C. 10 − 2 = 28	D. 19 − 5 = 14	E. 14 − 5 = 9
F. 16 − 4 = 12	G. 19 − 2 = 17	H. 21 − 7 = 14	I. 40 − 5 = 35	J. 62 − 9 = 53
K. 28 − 16 = 12	L. 38 − 12 = 26	M. 42 − 7 = 35	N. 46 − 25 = 21	O. 28 − 14 = 14

Analogies

Fill in the blanks to complete the **analogies**.

1. A **mouth** is to **taste** as an eye is to   **see**
2. A **person** is to a **house** as a bear is to a   **cave**
3. An **apple** is to a **tree** as a watermelon is to a   **vine**
4. A **kitten** is to a **cat** as a puppy is to a   **dog**
5. An **inch** is to **length** as a pound is to   **weight**
6. A **car** is to a **road** as a boat is to   **water**
7. A **whale** is to **water** as an elephant is to   **land**

48

Nouns and Verbs

Read each sentence below. Underline each **noun**. Circle each **verb**.

1. Ryan and Cathy _went_ to the museum.
2. Beverly _washes_ the big, green car.
3. The big, black dog _scared_ Chris.
4. Wanda _lives_ in Georgia.
5. Don _owns_ a large store.
6. The warm night _was_ peaceful.
7. The girl _was_ late for practice.
8. Brian _put_ the blue sweater in the dryer.
9. Amber _had_ fun at the park.

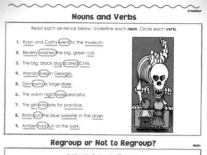

Regroup or Not to Regroup?

Subtract to find each difference.

A. 63 − 21 = 42	B. 45 − 25 = 20	C. 75 − 23 = 52	D. 33 − 11 = 22	E. 46 − 21 = 25
F. 32 − 15 = 17	G. 55 − 27 = 28	H. 90 − 42 = 48	I. 75 − 68 = 7	J. 35 − 16 = 19

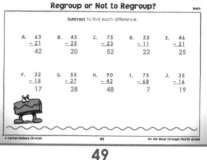

49

Building Vocabulary

Davey has a new friend who keeps bothering him. Read the story to find out more. Then, read each of the five sentences. Write the letter for the best answer on the line.

A Fishing Friend

It all began last summer when Davey was fishing at his grandpa's farm. Suddenly, something odd **occurred**. A big head **emerged** from the water. Davey was **terrified** at first. The creature smiled and told Davey that his name was Clarence.

Clarence told Davey that he had always been alone and was tired of his **solitude**. He wanted a friend. Davey felt sorry for Clarence and tried his best to cheer him up.

Now it seems that Davey has a friend for life. There's just one problem: Clarence wants to be with Davey all the time. Davey can't go fishing alone anymore. He hopes Clarence will find another new friend soon. Davey would like some of his own solitude. He would also like to catch some fish. Few fish come around when Clarence is near!

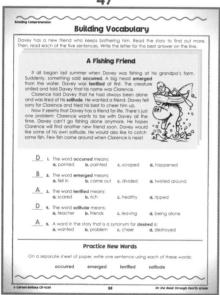

D 1. The word **occurred** means:
    a. pointed **b.** painted **c.** scraped **d.** happened

B 2. The word **emerged** means:
    a. fell in **b.** came out **c.** divided **d.** twisted around

A 3. The word **terrified** means:
    a. scared **b.** rich **c.** healthy **d.** ripped

D 4. The word **solitude** means:
    a. teacher **b.** friends **c.** leaving **d.** being alone

A 5. A word in the story that is a synonym for **desired** is:
    a. wanted **b.** problem **c.** cheer **d.** destroyed

Practice New Words

On a separate sheet of paper, write one sentence using each of these words:

occurred   emerged   terrified   solitude

50

Beat the Clock (Double-Digit Subtraction)

Make several copies of this page. Time yourself every day for a week. Does your time improve? Does your accuracy increase?

A. 86 − 58 = 28	90 − 29 = 61	42 − 28 = 14	94 − 66 = 28	62 − 49 = 13	55 − 17 = 38	41 − 25 = 16
B. 75 − 17 = 58	47 − 18 = 29	40 − 29 = 11	54 − 23 = 31	54 − 38 = 16	81 − 27 = 54	67 − 38 = 29
C. 91 − 56 = 35	52 − 49 = 3	43 − 38 = 5	71 − 34 = 37	75 − 46 = 29	84 − 47 = 37	61 − 12 = 49
D. 93 − 75 = 18	84 − 19 = 65	82 − 73 = 9	84 − 37 = 47	66 − 48 = 18	75 − 27 = 48	54 − 39 = 15
E. 87 − 38 = 49	74 − 25 = 49	67 − 38 = 29	71 − 64 = 7	83 − 28 = 55	41 − 34 = 7	71 − 42 = 29

Time: _____   Number correct: _____

51

More Nouns and Verbs

Look at the words in the word list. Write the **nouns** on the building. Write the **verbs** on the rocket.

Word List

pretend
news
remove
school
cow
be
earth
flee
sell
lamp
car
took
speak
hear
berry
lake
bring
heart
window
understand
easel
wear

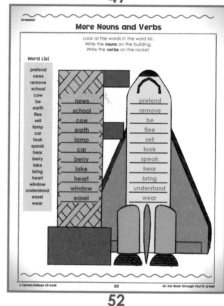

Building (nouns): news, school, cow, earth, lamp, car, berry, lake, heart, window, easel

Rocket (verbs): pretend, remove, be, flee, sell, took, speak, hear, bring, understand, wear

52

Plurals (-s or -es)

Add the correct ending (**s** or **es**) to make each word **plural**. Write the new words on the lines.

1. teacher — teachers
2. potato — potatoes
3. house — houses
4. kite — kites
5. class — classes
6. clown — clowns
7. box — boxes
8. handbook — handbooks
9. watch — watches
10. friend — friends
11. clock — clocks
12. computer — computers
13. couch — couches
14. carmel — carmels
15. fox — foxes

Adding & Subtracting with Decimals

Add or **subtract** to solve each problem.

A. 7.0 + 7.5 = 14.5	B. 9.2 − 4.1 = 5.1	C. 8.3 − 2.8 = 5.5
D. 23.5 − 16.3 = 7.2	E. 4.23 + 1.95 = 6.18	F. 6.35 − 4.96 = 1.39
G. 2.98 + 6.85 = 9.83	H. 96.3 − 21.4 = 74.9	I. 6.91 + 2.98 = 9.89

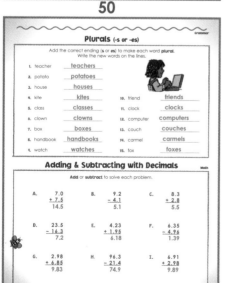

53

Story Problems

Solve each word problem.

A. Shannon bought 3 dozen eggs at the store. On the way home, she dropped the egg cartons and 13 of the eggs broke. How many unbroken eggs does Shannon now have?   36 − 13 = 23

B. Dawn is allowed to swim in the pool for 60 minutes each day. If she has been swimming today for 25 minutes, how many more minutes does she have left in the pool?   60 − 25 = 35

C. There were 937 students at Ridge Hill School. If 43 students missed school due to illness, how many students were at school?   937 − 43 = 894

D. Phil's Used Car Lot had 142 cars to sell. If Phil sold 26 of the cars, how many did he have left to sell?   142 − 26 = 116

E. Together, Cindy and Jim counted 221 cars on their road trip. Cindy counted 132 of the cars. How many cars did Jim count?   221 − 132 = 89

Categories

Read each group of words or phrases. Choose the best category name from the box. Write the correct category under each list. The first one has been done for you.

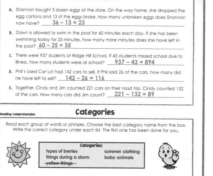

Categories:
types of berries   summer clothing
things during a storm   baby animals
yellow things

1.	2.	3.	4.
A. sun	A. bathing suit	A. strawberry	A. foal
B. banana	B. sunglasses	B. raspberry	B. lamb
C. daisy	C. shorts	C. blackberry	C. chick
D. corn	D. sandals	D. blueberry	D. duckling
E. lemon	E. short-sleeved shirt	E. boysenberry	E. kitten

Category: yellow things   Category: summer clothing   Category: types of berries   Category: baby animals

54

Possessive Plurals

Make each highlighted word **possessive** by rewriting the word on the line and adding an apostrophe in the correct place.

1. That is **Danas** dollhouse.   Dana's
2. **Craigs** truck is very big.   Craig's
3. I like **Sharons** new green bicycle.   Sharon's
4. The **childrens** song was perfectly in tune.   children's
5. The two **girls** kites flew high in the sky.   girls'
6. The **schools** end-of-the-year picnic was fun.   school's
7. The **trucks** loud horn scared Barbara.   truck's
8. The **actors** costume was colorful.   actor's
9. I love to visit my **grandmothers** house.   grandmother's
10. The **singers** voices are beautiful.   singers'
11. Those **dogs** collars are green.   dogs'

Three- and Four-Digit Subtraction

Subtract to solve each problem. Circle the smallest answer. Draw a square around the largest answer.

A. 912 − 735 = 177	B. 583 − 321 = 262	C. 185 − 112 = 73	D. 635 − 504 = 131
E. 865 − 125 = 740	F. 999 − 428 = 571	G. 2,190 − 1,065 = 1,125	H. 5,948 − 2,374 = 3,574

55

Answer Key

Page 56

Three-Digit Subtraction

Subtract to solve each problem. Circle all the even numbers.

A.
423 − 285 = (138)
222 − 153 = 69
435 − 166 = 269
628 − 499 = 129
757 − 178 = 579
637 − 388 = 249
423 − 285 = (138)

B.
326 − 285 = 41
972 − 609 = 363
685 − 246 = 439
518 − 329 = 189
741 − 362 = 379
438 − 258 = (180)
371 − 283 = 88

C.
529 − 482 = 47
625 − 407 = (218)
514 − 126 = (388)
664 − 278 = (386)
742 − 467 = 275
200 − 158 = (42)
634 − 277 = 357

Adjectives

Underline the adjectives in each paragraph below.
The first adjective has been underlined for you.

1. I like chocolate ice cream. Chocolate ice cream tastes good when it is hot outside. Unfortunately, chocolate ice cream makes a big, sticky mess. I solve this problem by eating my yummy, chocolate ice cream outside.

2. One sunny day, I found a white rabbit hopping in front of my house. I walked up to the frightened rabbit and talked to him. He finally calmed down and I picked him up. His soft fur tickled my hands. I took the sweet rabbit behind my house to the big forest. Waiting there for him was his happy mother. the two small rabbits hopped home together.

56

Page 57

Persuasive Paragraph

You must convince your mom to let you go bowling.
Ask her, give your reasons, and then ask again.

Title of paragraph: _____

Question: May I _____

Reasons:
1. _____
2. Answers will vary.
3. _____
4. _____

Ask again: _____

Use the information above to write a paragraph. Ask the question. State the reasons, and then ask the question again. Indent the first sentence. Use capital letters and periods. Remember to give your paragraph a title.

Answers will vary.

57

Page 58

Abbreviations

Write the correct abbreviation for each word on the line next to it.
Use a dictionary to check your answers for spelling and capitalization.

Street — St.   pound — lb.   minute — min.
Junior — Jr.   ounce — oz.   foot — ft.
Mister — Mr.   Senior — Sr.   inch — in.
Doctor — Dr.   centimeter — cm President — Pres.
Apartment — Apt. Road — Rd.   Mountain — Mt.

Subtraction Review

Subtract to solve each problem.

A.
623 − 194 = 429
900 − 309 = 591
722 − 317 = 405
377 − 186 = 191
871 − 384 = 487
628 − 300 = 328

B.
990 − 731 = 259
818 − 693 = 125
572 − 335 = 237
951 − 357 = 594
825 − 469 = 356
771 − 217 = 554

Write the answers in order from smallest to largest.

125   191   237   259   328   356
405   429   487   554   591   594

58

Page 59

Subtraction with Decimals

Subtract to solve each problem.

A. 20.20 − 13.75 = 6.45
B. 334.5 − 145.6 = 188.9
C. 7.051 − 2.058 = 4.993
D. 3.812 − 2.116 = 1.696
E. 8.229 − 2.443 = 5.786
F. 421.6 − 334.7 = 86.9

Contractions

Read each sentence. Circle the correct contraction for the highlighted words.

1. I did not look at the movie when it was scary! — (didn't) / did'nt / don't
2. You are my best friend! — You'd / You'll / (You're)
3. Are you sure we are on the right path? — we'd / we'll / (we're)
4. Brian said he is older than you. — (he's) / he's / he'll
5. Who would want to live in that dusty old house? — (Who'd) / Who's / Who've
6. They are very kind people. — They'll / (They're) / They've
7. Let us begin the lesson. — Lets / (Let's) / Lets
8. You are going to be late for school. — Your'e / (You're) / Your
9. You have given me plenty of reasons to study. — You'd / You're / (You've)
10. I am going to the zoo tomorrow. — I'd / I'll / (I'm)

59

Page 60

Pronouns

Read each sentence. Replace the highlighted word(s) with the correct pronoun by writing it on the lines.

1. Jim and Carla like to ride motorcycles. _They_ ride whenever they can.
2. Jane has two lovebirds. _She_ sings to them every day.
3. Chelsea and Cheyna are sisters. Let's go to their house and play with _them_.
4. Billy is a police officer. _He_ likes to help people.
5. This book is from my grandparents. _It_ is my favorite.
6. Daphne and I like jelly beans. _We_ like to eat the red ones.
7. That is Rocky's baseball. Please give it to _him_.

Subtraction with Decimals

A. 8.5 − 2.8 = 5.7
B. 9.2 − 7.5 = 1.7
C. 7.1 − 4.1 = 3.0
D. 3.75 − 2.12 = 1.63
E. 54.3 − 19.4 = 34.9
F. 9.35 − 5.68 = 3.67
G. 2.01 − 1.95 = .06
H. 5.12 − 4.08 = 1.04
I. 53.0 − 22.6 = 30.4

If the answers were dollar amounts, which problem would you like? [E]

60

Page 61

Building Vocabulary

Ike and Spike are two young boys. Read the story to find out some of the messes they get themselves involved in. Then, read each of the five sentences. Write the letter for the best answer on the line.

Ike, Spike, and the Circle Game

Ike and Spike are two brave little boys who will try anything once. There's just one problem. These eight-year-old friends can never agree. They always want to do things in different ways. That's quite a dilemma sometimes!

Once they created a large mural. Ike's faces were smiling, and Spike's faces all frowned. Another day, the boys went for a long hike. Ike took the path up into the hills, and Spike walked down by the river. They didn't find each other again until the next day.

Here you see them struggling to get home from a fishing excursion. Each boy wants to go a different way. These poor guys have been spinning in circles for an hour. Maybe soon one will get tired so they can at least move the boat!

B 1. The word dilemma means:
   a. canoe   b. problem   c. bait   d. song

A 2. The word created means:
   a. made   b. heard   c. told   d. found

C 3. The word struggling means:
   a. laughing   b. running   c. trying hard   d. painting

C 4. The word excursion means:
   a. hat   b. lesson   c. trip   d. fort

D 5. A word in the story that is a synonym for varied is:
   a. ordinary   b. poor   c. problem   d. different

Practice New Words

On a separate sheet of paper, write one sentence using each of these words.

dilemma   created   struggling   excursion

61

Page 62

Mixed Problems with Decimals

Add or subtract to solve each problem.

A. 726.6 + 122.5 = 849.1
B. 9.025 − 1.874 = 7.151
C. 423.8 + 111.4 = 535.2
D. 8.345 + 2.137 = 10.482
E. 77.61 − 44.32 = 33.29
F. 522.7 + 311.7 = 834.4

List the answers from largest to smallest.

849.1
834.4
535.2
33.29
10.482
7.151

Using Guide Words

Look at the words in the word list. Print each word in alphabetical order below the two guide words it would appear between in a dictionary.

1. aardvark — afghan
   aboard
   about
   above
   affect
   afford

2. Africa — aim
   after
   aggravate
   agree
   aid
   ailment

Word List
aggravate
above
aboard
affect
about
after
aid
agree
ailment
afford

62

Page 63

Understanding What I've Read

Parasites

Some animals get their food by living in or on other things. These animals, called parasites, do not kill the animals they live on, but they may harm or irritate them. A flea will live on a dog, cat, or other animals. The animal it lives on is called the host. The flea gets its food by sucking the other animal's blood. The flea will not harm the host, but it will make the host itch and feel uncomfortable. Some worms are also parasites. A tapeworm lives inside the body of an animal. It eats the food the host has eaten. The tapeworm can make the host very sick. Plants can be parasites, too. Mistletoe and some types of ferns live on trees, taking food and water from them.

1. What is the main idea of this story?
   a. (Parasites live on or in other living things.)
   b. A flea is a parasite.
   c. Parasites can make their hosts sick.

2. How does a flea get food?
   It sucks its host's blood.

3. Where does a tapeworm live?
   It lives inside the body of an animal.

4. What is a parasite?
   It is an animal that lives and feeds in or on other things.

5. What does the word host mean?
   a. an animal that lives on another living thing
   b. (the animal a parasite lives on)
   c. mistletoe

6. What kinds of plants can be parasites?
   Mistletoe and some ferns

63

Page 64

Beat the Clock (Multiplication Facts 0 to 4)

A.
7 × 4 = 28
4 × 6 = 24
1 × 3 = 3
9 × 5 = 45
4 × 1 = 4
4 × 8 = 32
6 × 1 = 6
8 × 6 = 48
3 × 0 = 0
5 × 5 = 25

B.
8 × 1 = 8
4 × 0 = 0
0 × 3 = 0
3 × 4 = 12
5 × 3 = 15
6 × 3 = 18
7 × 3 = 21
1 × 0 = 0
9 × 8 = 72
2 × 7 = 14

C.
5 × 4 = 20
2 × 0 = 0
8 × 7 = 56
0 × 4 = 0
5 × 1 = 5
4 × 7 = 28
0 × 6 = 0
3 × 3 = 9
8 × 3 = 24
0 × 1 = 0

D.
7 × 1 = 7
4 × 9 = 36
6 × 7 = 42
9 × 0 = 0
0 × 7 = 0
9 × 5 = 45
6 × 7 = 42
3 × 1 = 3
4 × 3 = 12

E.
0 × 9 = 0
5 × 8 = 40
1 × 6 = 6
5 × 6 = 30
1 × 1 = 1
9 × 4 = 36
4 × 1 = 4
3 × 4 = 12
5 × 4 = 20

F.
7 × 7 = 49
3 × 9 = 27
1 × 5 = 5
0 × 0 = 0
6 × 6 = 36
4 × 1 = 4
3 × 4 = 12
8 × 3 = 24
1 × 0 = 0
5 × 2 = 10

G.
9 × 3 = 27
1 × 9 = 9
7 × 0 = 0
4 × 4 = 16
0 × 5 = 0
5 × 8 = 40
9 × 9 = 81
2 × 2 = 4
8 × 8 = 64
1 × 3 = 3

H.
2 × 8 = 16
1 × 6 = 6
9 × 6 = 54
1 × 7 = 7
7 × 5 = 35
4 × 8 = 32
0 × 8 = 0
9 × 8 = 72
7 × 3 = 21
9 × 7 = 63

I.
5 × 7 = 35
8 × 8 = 64
4 × 6 = 24
9 × 1 = 9
5 × 3 = 15
2 × 9 = 18
6 × 8 = 48
7 × 2 = 14
1 × 2 = 2
9 × 7 = 63

J.
8 × 2 = 16
3 × 6 = 18
0 × 7 = 0
7 × 8 = 56
1 × 0 = 10
9 × 2 = 18
3 × 6 = 18
9 × 6 = 54
1 × 8 = 8
5 × 6 = 30

Time: _____   Number correct: _____

64

Answer Key

Antonyms, Synonyms, and Homonyms

Use the clues below to solve the **crossword puzzle**.

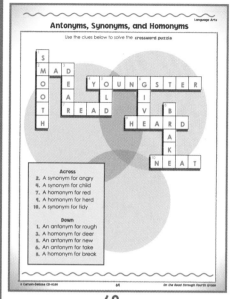

Crossword answers:
- S M A D (MAD)
- YOUNGSTER
- READ
- HEARD
- NEAT

Across
2. A synonym for angry
4. A synonym for child
7. A homonym for red
9. A homonym for herd
10. A synonym for tidy

Down
1. An antonym for rough
3. A homonym for deer
5. An antonym for new
6. An antonym for take
8. A homonym for break

Page 69

Multiplication Facts

Fill in the numbers to complete the facts.

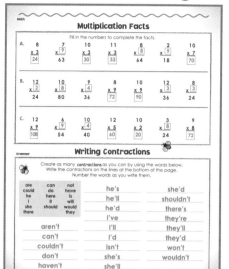

A.
8	9	11	8	9	10
x 3	x 7	x 3	x 8	x 2	x 7
24	63	33	64	18	70

B.
12	10	9	8	9	12
x 2	x 8	x 4	x 9	x 9	x 3
24	80	36	72	90	36	24

C.
12	6	10	10	3	9
x 9	x 9	x 4	x 2	x 8	x 8
108	54	40	60	20	24	72

Writing Contractions

Create as many **contractions** as you can by using the words below.
Write the contractions on the lines at the bottom of the page.
Number the words as you write them.

are	can	not
could	do	have
I	has	is
she	it	will
there	should	would
		they

he's, he'll, he'd, I've, aren't, can't, couldn't, don't, haven't — she'd, shouldn't, there's, they're, I'll, I'd, isn't, she's, she'll — they'll, they'd, won't, wouldn't

Page 70

Prefixes

Use the prefix bank and word list to **create as many words as you can**.
Write the words on the lines. Use another sheet of paper if needed.

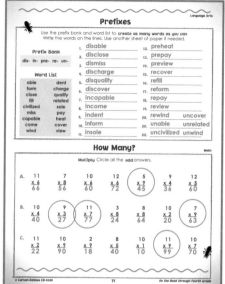

Prefix Bank
dis- in- pre- re- un-

Word List
able, form, close, fill, civilized, miss, capable, come, wind — dent, charge, qualify, related, sole, pay, heal, cover, view

1. disable
2. disclose
3. dismiss
4. discharge
5. disqualify
6. discover
7. incapable
8. income
9. indent
10. inform
11. insole
12. preheat
13. prepay
14. preview
15. recover
16. refill
17. reform
18. repay
19. review
20. rewind   uncover
21. unable   unrelated
22. uncivilized   unwind

How Many?

Multiply. Circle all the **odd** answers.

A.
11	7	10	12	(5)	9	12
x 6	x 8	x 6	x 6	x 9	x 4	x 5
66	56	60	72	45	36	60

B.
10	(9)	(11)	3	8	10	(7)
x 4	x 3	x 7	x 8	x 8	x 2	x 9
40	27	77	24	64	20	63

C.
11	10	2	10	10	(11)	10
x 2	x 9	x 9	x 5	x 1	x 9	x 7
22	90	18	50	10	99	70

Page 71

Building Vocabulary

Gordy the gorilla and Tussie the elephant are good friends. Read the story to learn more about one of their adventures. Then, read each of the five sentences. Write the letter for the best answer on the line.

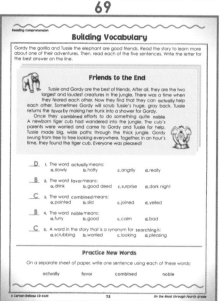

Friends to the End

Tussie and Gordy are the best of friends. After all, they are the two largest and loudest creatures in the jungle. There was a time when they feared each other. Now they find that they can actually help each other. Sometimes Gordy will scrub Tussie's huge, gray back. Tussie returns the favor by making her trunk into a shower for Gordy.

Once they **combined** efforts to do something quite **noble**. A newborn tiger cub had wandered into the jungle. The cub's parents were worried and came to Gordy and Tussie for help. Tussie made big, wide paths through the thick jungle. Gordy swung from tree to tree looking everywhere. Together, in an hour's time, they found the tiger cub. Everyone was pleased!

D 1. The word **actually** means:
   a. slowly b. hotly c. angrily d. really

B 2. The word **favor** means:
   a. drink b. good deed c. surprise d. dark night

C 3. The word **combined** means:
   a. pointed b. slid c. joined d. yelled

B 4. The word **noble** means:
   a. furry b. good c. calm d. bad

C 5. A word in the story that is a synonym for **searching** is:
   a. scrubbing b. worried c. looking d. pleasing

Practice New Words

On a separate sheet of paper, write one sentence using each of these words.

actually   favor   combined   noble

Page 72

Find the Missing Factors

Write the missing **factor** to complete each fact.

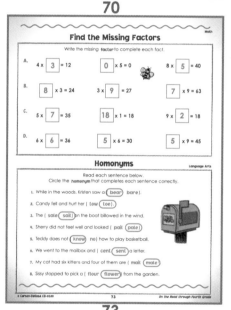

A. 4 x 3 = 12   0 x 5 = 0   8 x 5 = 40
B. 8 x 3 = 24   3 x 9 = 27   7 x 9 = 63
C. 5 x 7 = 35   18 x 1 = 18   9 x 2 = 18
D. 6 x 6 = 36   5 x 6 = 30   5 x 9 = 45

Homonyms

Read each sentence below.
Circle the **homonym** that completes each sentence correctly.

1. While in the woods, Kristen saw a (**bear** bare).
2. Candy fell and hurt her (**toe** tow).
3. The (sale **sail**) on the boat billowed in the wind.
4. Sherry did not feel well and looked (pail **pale**).
5. Teddy does not (**know** no) how to play basketball.
6. We went to the mailbox to (cent **sent**) a letter.
7. My cat has six kittens and four of them are (mail **male**).
8. Sissy stopped to pick a (flour **flower**) from the garden.

Page 73

Multiplication Word Problems

Use **multiplication** to solve each word problem.

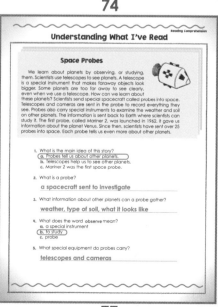

A. Stephen, Wendy, and Spencer each spent $9 at the amusement park. How much money did they spend altogether? $ **27**

B. Jennifer likes to make dolls. If she makes 3 dolls each day for 6 days, how many dolls will she have made? **18** dolls

C. Tory keeps his race cars in shoe boxes. He has 11 boxes with 5 cars in each. How many race cars does Tory have? **55** race cars

D. Tamika rode her bike for 2 hours every day for 8 days. How many hours did she ride altogether in those 8 days? **16** hours

E. Justin, Dylan, and Stephanie all wear hats. If they each have 12 hats, how many hats do they have altogether? **36** hats

F. Ursula had 3 mother cats. Each mother cat had 5 kittens. How many kittens did Ursula's cats have altogether? **15** kittens

G. Sean collects postage stamps. He puts 12 stamps on each page of his album. If Sean has 8 filled pages, how many stamps does Sean have? **96** stamps

H. Denise built 7 towers with building blocks. If she used 8 blocks for each tower, how many blocks did she use in all? **56** blocks

I. Gina wants to make friendship necklaces. She will use 9 beads on each necklace. How many beads does Gina need to make 5 necklaces? **45** beads

Page 74

Compare and Contrast

Fill in the blanks to compare and contrast a newspaper and a book. The first one has been done for you.

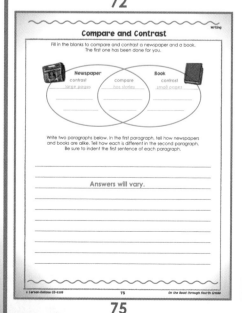

Newspaper
contrast: large pages

compare: has stories

Book
contrast: small pages

Write two paragraphs below. In the first paragraph, tell how newspapers and books are alike. Tell how each is different in the second paragraph. Be sure to indent the first sentence of each paragraph.

Answers will vary.

Page 75

Match the Fact to the Answer

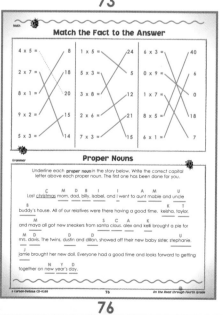

4 x 5	8
2 x 7	18
8 x 1	20
9 x 2	15
5 x 3	14

1 x 5	24
5 x 3	9
3 x 8	12
2 x 6	21
7 x 3	15

6 x 3	40
0 x 9	9
1 x 7	0
8 x 5	18
6 x 1	7

Proper Nouns

Underline each **proper noun** in the story below. Write the correct capital letter above each proper noun. The first one has been done for you.

Last christmas mom, dad, billy, isabel, and I went to aunt mable and uncle buddy's house. All of our relatives were there having a good time. keisha, taylor, and maya all got new sneakers from santa claus. alex and kelli brought a pie for mrs. davis. The twins, dustin and dillon, showed off their new baby sister, stephanie. jamie brought her new doll. Everyone had a good time and looks forward to getting together on new year's day.

Page 76

Understanding What I've Read

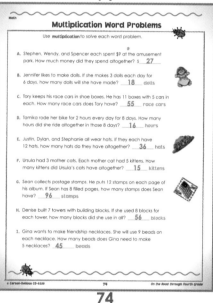

Space Probes

We learn about planets by observing, or studying, them. Scientists use telescopes to see planets. A telescope is a special instrument that makes faraway objects look bigger. Some planets are too far away to see clearly, even when we use a telescope. How can we learn about these planets? Scientists send special spacecraft called probes into space. Telescopes and cameras are sent in the probe to record everything they see. Probes also carry special instruments to examine the weather and soil on other planets. The information is sent back to Earth where scientists can study it. The first probe, called Mariner 2, was launched in 1962. It gave us information about the planet Venus. Since then, scientists have sent over 25 probes into space. Each probe tells us even more about other planets.

1. What is the main idea of this story?
   a. Probes tell us about other planets.
   b. Telescopes help us to see other planets.
   c. Mariner 2 was the first space probe.

2. What is a probe?
   a spacecraft sent to investigate

3. What information about other planets can a probe gather?
   weather, type of soil, what it looks like

4. What does the word observe mean?
   a. a special instrument
   b. to study
   c. probe

5. What special equipment do probes carry?
   telescopes and cameras

Page 77

Answer Key

A Multiplication Puzzle

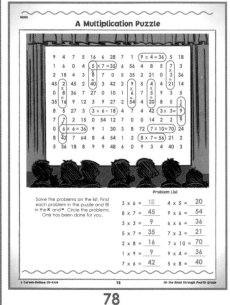

Solve the problems on the list. Find each problem in the puzzle and fill in the **x** and **=**. Circle the problems. One has been done for you.

Problem List

3 x 6 = **18**   4 x 5 = **20**
8 x 7 = **45**   9 x 6 = **54**
3 x 3 = **9**   6 x 6 = **36**
5 x 7 = **35**   7 x 3 = **21**
2 x 8 = **16**   7 x 10 = **70**
1 x 9 = **9**   9 x 4 = **36**
7 x 6 = **42**   5 x 8 = **40**

78

Descriptive Writing

The three adjectives below describe the picture. Add two more adjectives of your own. Write a paragraph about the picture using these adjectives. Remember to indent the first sentence of your paragraph and to include a title.

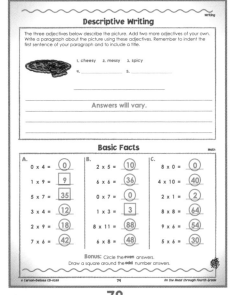

1. cheesy   2. messy   3. spicy

4.   5.

Answers will vary.

Basic Facts

A.		B.		C.	
0 x 4 =	**0**	2 x 5 =	**10**	8 x 0 =	**0**
1 x 9 =	**9**	6 x 6 =	**36**	4 x 10 =	**40**
5 x 7 =	**35**	0 x 7 =	**0**	2 x 1 =	**2**
3 x 4 =	**12**	1 x 3 =	**3**	8 x 8 =	**64**
2 x 9 =	**18**	8 x 11 =	**88**	9 x 6 =	**54**
7 x 6 =	**42**	6 x 8 =	**48**	5 x 6 =	**30**

Bonus: Circle the **even** answers.
Draw a square around the **odd** number answers.

79

One-Digit Times Two-Digit Multiplication

Multiply to solve the problems.

A.
21 x 9 = 189   70 x 0 = 0   42 x 3 = 126   76 x 6 = 456

B.
98 x 1 = 98   61 x 2 = 122   21 x 4 = 84   22 x 2 = 44

C.
64 x 4 = 256   29 x 5 = 145   38 x 7 = 266   56 x 9 = 504

Punctuation Review

Add the correct **punctuation** at the end of each sentence.

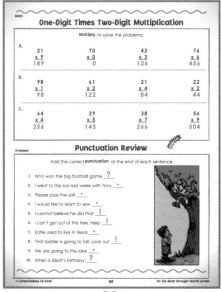

1. Who won the big football game **?**
2. I went to the zoo last week with Tony **.**
3. Please pass the salt **.**
4. I would like to learn to sew **.**
5. I cannot believe he did that **!**
6. I can't get out of this tree. Help **!**
7. Katie used to live in Texas **.**
8. That ladder is going to fall. Look out **!**
9. We are going to the lake **.**
10. When is Elliott's birthday **?**

80

Sequencing Events

Read the story to learn about the old house. Then, read the sentences below. Decide what happened first, second, and so on. Number the sentences in the correct order.

The Old House

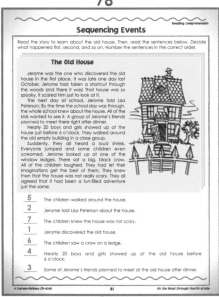

Jerome was the one who discovered the old house in the first place. It was late one day last October. Jerome had taken a shortcut through the woods and there it was! That house was so spooky, it scared him just to look at it.

The next day at school, Jerome told Lisa Peterson. By the time the school day was through, the whole school knew about the house. All of the kids wanted to see it. A group of Jerome's friends planned to meet there right after dinner.

Nearly 20 boys and girls showed up at the house just before 6 o'clock. They walked around the old empty building in a close group.

Suddenly, they all heard a loud shriek. Everyone jumped and some children even screamed. Jerome looked up at one of the window ledges. There sat a big, black crow. All of the children laughed. They had let their imaginations get the best of them. They knew then that the house was not really scary. They all agreed that it had been a fun-filled adventure just the same.

5 The children walked around the house.
2 Jerome told Lisa Peterson about the house.
7 The children knew the house was not scary.
1 Jerome discovered the old house.
6 The children saw a crow on a ledge.
4 Nearly 20 boys and girls showed up at the old house before 6 o'clock.
3 Some of Jerome's friends planned to meet at the old house after dinner.

81

One-Digit Times Three-Digit Multiplication

Multiply to solve the problems.

A. 173 x 3 = 519   B. 452 x 2 = 904   C. 168 x 5 = 840   D. 223 x 6 = 1,338

E. 180 x 5 = 900   F. 232 x 4 = 928   G. 549 x 2 = 1,098   H. 257 x 8 = 2,056

Write the answers in order from smallest to largest.

519   840   900   904   928   1,098   1,338   2,056

Combining Root Words and Suffixes

Use the suffix bank and the word list to **create as many words as you can**. Write the words on the lines at the bottom of the page. Remember to change the **y** to an **i** when adding a suffix. Use another sheet of paper if needed.

Suffix Bank
-er   -ful   -less
-ly   -ness

Word List
teach   thought
beauty   boast
doubt   shy
happy   bake
sad   care
quick   friend
awkward   help
peace   law
quiet   wonder

1. awkwardly   12. sadness
2. baker   13. shyness
3. beautiful   14. teacher
4. boastful   15. thoughtful
5. careful   16. wonderful
6. doubtful   17.
7. friendly   18.
8. happiness   19.
9. helpless   20.
10. peaceful   21.
11. quietly   22.
                      23.

Answers will vary.

82

Compound Words

Fill in each blank with a word from the word list to make a **compound word**. Use each word only once.

Word List   boat   shore   case   fly   nap   bug
                board   burger   crow   coat   book   time

scare **crow**   night **time**
cook **book**   cheese **burger**
cat **nap**   sea **shore**
steam **boat**   horse **fly**
suit **case**   chalk **board**
rain **coat**   lady **bug**

Story Problems

Solve each word problem.

A. The Super Coaster roller coaster ride has 15 cars. Each car has 4 seats. How many people can ride the Super Coaster at one time?
60 people

B. Last week, 21 mother dogs had puppies. If they each had 6 puppies, how many puppies did the dogs have altogether? **126 puppies**

C. Cheri can make 32 bracelets a week. She made bracelets for 12 weeks. How many bracelets did Cheri make? **384 bracelets**

D. Sixteen packages of crayons were donated to Mr. Horowitz's class. Each package had 64 crayons. How many crayons were donated in all?
1,024 crayons

83

Greater Than or Less Than?

Multiply to solve the problems. Write **>** or **<** in the box to show if the first answer is greater or less than the second answer.

A. 159 x 8 = 1,272   **>**   221 x 5 = 1,105
B. 983 x 3 = 2,949   **<**   759 x 4 = 3,036
C. 865 x 1 = 865   **<**   182 x 7 = 1,274
D. 135 x 9 = 1,215   **>**   203 x 5 = 1,015
E. 315 x 4 = 1,260   **<**   275 x 6 = 1,650
F. 249 x 2 = 498   **<**   259 x 3 = 777

Using Synonyms

Read each sentence. Replace the word in parentheses with a **synonym**. Write the synonym on the line.

Answers will vary.

1. Rascal is a (small) _____ dog.
2. Timmy can run (fast) _____.
3. Did you (complete) _____ your homework?
4. I like to (yell) _____ when I am outside.
5. That box is an (odd) _____ color.
6. Will your mother (allow) _____ us to eat pizza?
7. My father brought me a (present) _____.
8. Kelly is wearing a (pretty) _____ dress.
9. Sonja recycled her (ancient) _____ letters.
10. The cat slept (below) _____ the table.
11. Patty likes to (converse) _____ with her friends.

84

Synonym Search

Match each pair of synonyms in the box below by connecting a word from the first column to a word in the second column. Then, find and circle each synonym pair in the word search. (Hint: Each pair of words is spelled across or down and does not share any letters.)

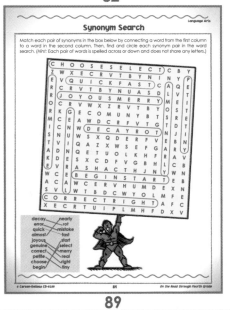

decay — rot
error — mistake
quick — fast
almost — nearly
joyous — merry
genuine — real
correct — right
petite — tiny
choose — select
begin — start

89

Interpreting a Grid

The children in Mr. Price's class made a **grid** showing the pets they own. Each check mark stands for one pet owned by a child. Use the grid to answer the questions.

Pets Owned by Mr. Price's Students

	Keisha	Juan	Maria	Tim	Anthony
turtle		√			√
rabbit	√	√			
snake					
lizard			√	√	
mouse	√	√			
fish			√	√	√
cat	√	√	√		√
dog		√		√	

A. What is the total number of pets listed on the grid? **21**
B. Which child owns the most pets? **Juan**
C. Which type of pet is owned by every child? **cat**
D. How many children own turtles? **2**
E. How many more pets does Maria have than Tim? **1**
F. Does Anthony have a pet turtle? **yes** a rabbit? **no**
G. What pets does Juan not own? **snake, lizard**

90

Answer Key

Finish the Sentences
Reading Comprehension

Read each sentence. Using the word list below, fill in each blank with a word that means the same as the highlighted word in each sentence.

Word List
totally, absent, detest, talented, error, increase, uncomfortable, strange, remain, companion

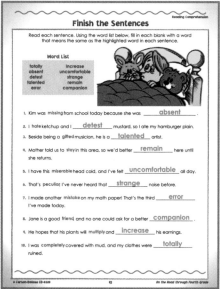

1. Kim was missing from school today because she was **absent**.
2. I hate ketchup and I **detest** mustard, so I ate my hamburger plain.
3. Beside being a gifted musician, he is a **talented** artist.
4. Mother told us to stay in this area, so we'd better **remain** here until she returns.
5. I have this miserable head cold, and I've felt **uncomfortable** all day.
6. That's peculiar, I've never heard that **strange** noise before.
7. I made another mistake on my math paper! That's the third **error** I've made today.
8. Jane is a good friend, and no one could ask for a better **companion**.
9. He hopes that his plants will multiply and **increase** his earnings.
10. I was completely covered with mud, and my clothes were **totally** ruined.

91

Show Your Work
Math

Multiply to solve each problem.

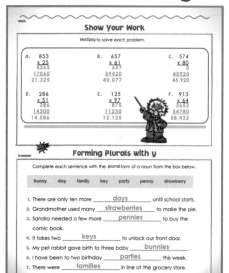

A. 853 × 25 4265 1706 **21,325**	B. 657 × 61 657 3942 **40,077**	C. 574 × 80 0 4592 **45,920**
D. 286 × 51 286 1430 **14,586**	E. 125 × 97 875 1125 **12,125**	F. 913 × 64 3652 5478 **58,432**

Forming Plurals with y
Grammar

Complete each sentence with the plural form of a noun from the box below.

bunny   day   family   key   party   penny   strawberry

1. There are only ten more **days** until school starts.
2. Grandmother used many **strawberries** to make the pie.
3. Sandra needed a few more **pennies** to buy the comic book.
4. It takes two **keys** to unlock our front door.
5. My pet rabbit gave birth to three baby **bunnies**.
6. I have been to two birthday **parties** this week.
7. There were **families** in line at the grocery store.

92

Forming Plurals with f
Grammar

Rewrite each word in the box as a plural on the line.

1. I would like to buy three **loaves** of bread.
2. Place the encyclopedias on those **shelves**.
3. The **calves** stood close to their mothers.
4. The **wolves** were hunting for food.
5. We wore our **scarves** outside in the snow.
6. A whole is made up of two **halves**.

loaf, shelf, calf, wolf, scarf, half

Show Your Work Again
Math

Multiply to solve each problem.

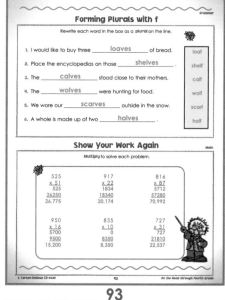

525 × 51 525 2625 **26,775**	917 × 22 1834 1834 **20,174**	816 × 87 5712 6528 **70,992**
950 × 16 5700 950 **15,200**	835 × 10 0 835 **8,350**	727 × 31 727 2181 **22,537**

93

What's Wrong?
Reading Comprehension

Read each paragraph. Underline the sentence in each paragraph that does not belong. The first one has been done for you.

1. Martha's dad is an electrician. He does many different kinds of things when he goes to work. Some days he checks the wiring in peoples' homes. Sometimes he checks the wiring in large buildings and shopping centers. ~~Martha is very proud of him.~~ He often helps put all the electrical wires and outlets in new buildings.

2. Jeremy has many reasons for wanting to be a dentist. He thinks having healthy teeth is very important. He has always been interested in all the things his own dentist does. Jeremy thinks he would be a good dentist, too. He has always enjoyed school.

3. Being a florist takes special training. You must know the names of all the flowers and plants. People who are in the hospital like to receive flowers. You must learn how to care for flowers and plants. It is also important to know how to arrange them.

4. Carl wants to be a teacher, but he can't decide what to teach. At first, he thought he would like to teach math. Then, he thought he would like to teach kindergarten. Carl likes many things. Now he thinks he would like to teach history.

How Much Money?
Math

Calculate the money in each piggy bank and print the total on the line. Use a dollar sign and a decimal point for each amount.

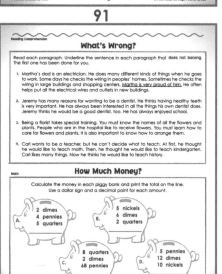

A. 2 dimes, 4 pennies, 5 quarters
B. 5 nickels, 6 dimes, 2 quarters
C. 8 quarters, 2 dimes, 68 pennies
D. 5 pennies, 2 dimes, 10 nickels

94

Contraction Fun
Language Arts

Rewrite the words below as contractions. Use the key to create a patchwork design pattern at the bottom of the page.

1. she will — **she'll**
2. you are — **you're**
3. he would — **he'd**
4. there is — **there's**
5. I am — **I'm**
6. can not — **can't**
7. they are — **they're**
8. should not — **shouldn't**
9. what is — **what's**
10. they will — **they'll**
11. we would — **we'd**
12. we are — **we're**

If the word ends in	Draw this pattern in the grid
'll	
're	
'd	
's	
'm	
't	

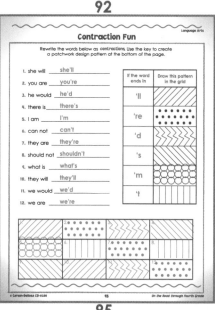

95

Solve the Code
Math

Multiply and solve the code to find out who wins the race. Use a calculator.

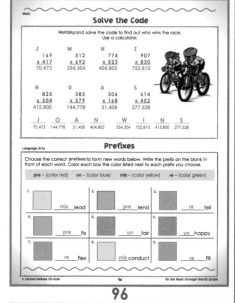

J	W	N	I
169 × 417 **70,473**	512 × 692 **354,304**	774 × 523 **404,802**	907 × 830 **752,810**

N	A	O	S
825 × 504 **415,800**	382 × 379 **144,778**	306 × 168 **51,408**	614 × 452 **277,528**

J O A N   W I N S
70,473 144,778 51,408 404,802   354,304 752,810 415,800 277,528

Prefixes
Language Arts

Choose the correct prefixes to form new words below. Write the prefix on the blank in front of each word. Color each box the color listed next to each prefix you choose.

pre – (color red)   un – (color blue)   mis – (color yellow)   re – (color green)

1. **mis** lead
2. **pre** tend
3. **re** tell
4. **pre** fix
5. **un** fair
6. **un** happy
7. **re** flex
8. **mis** conduct
9. **re** fill

96

Analogies
Language Arts

Compare the relationships of the words below. Find the missing word for each analogy and write it in the space provided.

1. in : out :: up : **down**
2. two : four :: three : **six**
3. snow : cold :: sun : **warm**
4. mother : aunt :: father : **uncle**
5. ear : hear :: eye : **see**
6. she : her :: he : **him**
7. dog : bark :: bird : **chirp**
8. brother : boy :: sister : **girl**
9. bear : den :: bee : **hive**
10. finger : hand :: toe : **foot**
11. girl : mother :: boy : **father**
12. left : right :: top : **bottom**

Learning to Divide
Math

Divide to solve each problem.

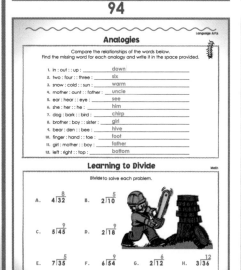

A. 4)32 = **8**
B. 2)10 = **5**
C. 5)45 = **9**
D. 2)18 = **9**
E. 7)35 = **5**
F. 6)54 = **9**
G. 2)12 = **6**
H. 3)36 = **12**

97

Division Designs
Math

Divide. Then connect the dots in order, beginning with the number given first.

Start at 5.
A. 45 ÷ 9 = 5
B. 12 ÷ 2 = 6
C. 36 ÷ 6 = 6
D. 6 ÷ 3 = 2
E. 8 ÷ 8 = 1
F. 35 ÷ 5 = 7
G. 7 ÷ 7 = 1

H. 24 ÷ 3 = 8
I. 42 ÷ 6 = 7
J. 6 ÷ 2 = 3
K. 27 ÷ 9 = 3
L. 2 ÷ 1 = 2
M. 54 ÷ 9 = 6

Start at 6.
A. 18 ÷ 3 = 6
B. 20 ÷ 4 = 5
C. 10 ÷ 5 = 2
D. 24 ÷ 4 = 6
E. 14 ÷ 2 = 7
F. 64 ÷ 8 = 8

G. 5 ÷ 5 = 1
H. 48 ÷ 8 = 6
I. 9 ÷ 9 = 1
J. 42 ÷ 7 = 6
K. 2 ÷ 2 = 1

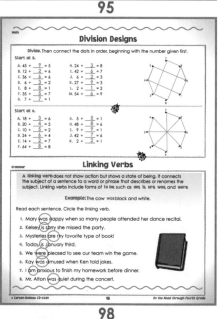

Linking Verbs
Grammar

A linking verb does not show action but shows a state of being. It connects the subject of a sentence to a word or phrase that describes or renames the subject. Linking verbs include forms of to be, such as am, is, are, was, and were.

Example: The cow was black and white.

Read each sentence. Circle the linking verb.

1. Mary (was) happy when so many people attended her dance recital.
2. Kelsey (is) sorry she missed the party.
3. Mysteries (are) my favorite type of book!
4. Today (is) January third.
5. We (were) pleased to see our team win the game.
6. Kay (was) amused when Ken told jokes.
7. I (am) anxious to finish my homework before dinner.
8. Mr. Alton (was) quiet during the concert.

98

Identifying Parts of Speech
Grammar

Read each sentence. Decide if the highlighted word is an adjective, an adverb, a noun, or a verb. Use the key to write Adj, Adv, N, or V, on the line.

Key
Adj – adjective   Adv – adverb   N – noun   V – verb

1. **Adj** The big red apple fell off the tree.
2. **N** The yellow dog followed Trina.
3. **V** Sarah fell down the stairs.
4. **N** Broccoli is on sale at the market today.
5. **Adv** Kenny slowly walked to school.
6. **Adj** My new sweater is very warm.
7. **V** Mariah sprinted across the meadow.
8. **Adj** The winner of the race cried tears of joy.
9. **N** The tornado did not damage our homes.

Story Problems
Math

Solve the story problems.

A. Patricia bought 16 doughnuts for herself and her 3 friends. If they each eat the same number of doughnuts, how many will each person eat? **4**

B. Catherine has 7 days to knit 21 sweaters. If she knits the same number of sweaters each day, how many will she have to make each day? **3**

C. Victoria picked 72 apples and used them to make pies. She used 6 apples in each pie. How many pies did Victoria make? **12**

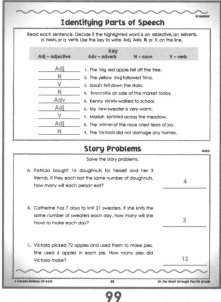

99

Answer Key

Descriptive Writing
Writing

Read the short paragraph.

> It was a nice day. Without warning, a storm suddenly blew in over the lake. We were afraid our boat would sink.

Here are some adjectives that can help describe the sentences:

What kind of day it was: **bright, sunny, lovely, warm, spring**
How the storm came in: **quickly, gusting, swirling, howling, thundering, booming**
What the storm looked like: **dark, cloudy, windy, blackness, inky**
What the people looked like: **pale, tense, worried, frightened**

Rewrite the paragraph to make it more colorful and interesting. Use the adjectives above or think of your own to describe what has happened in the paragraph. Give the paragraph a title.

Paragraphs will vary.

100

Beat the Clock (Division Facts 1 to 4)
Math

A.	36 ÷ 6 = 6	8 ÷ 1 = 8	45 ÷ 9 = 5	16 ÷ 8 = 2	35 ÷ 5 = 7
B.	24 ÷ 8 = 3	27 ÷ 9 = 3	20 ÷ 5 = 4	21 ÷ 3 = 7	8 ÷ 2 = 4
C.	20 ÷ 4 = 5	42 ÷ 7 = 6	18 ÷ 6 = 3	14 ÷ 2 = 7	28 ÷ 7 = 4
D.	56 ÷ 8 = 7	9 ÷ 3 = 3	3 ÷ 1 = 3	40 ÷ 8 = 5	12 ÷ 4 = 3
E.	10 ÷ 2 = 5	48 ÷ 6 = 8	45 ÷ 9 = 5	0 ÷ 6 = 0	15 ÷ 3 = 5
F.	7 ÷ 7 = 1	6 ÷ 2 = 3	18 ÷ 9 = 2	7 ÷ 1 = 7	32 ÷ 4 = 8
G.	5 ÷ 1 = 5	35 ÷ 5 = 7	56 ÷ 7 = 8	5 ÷ 5 = 0	30 ÷ 3 = 10
H.	18 ÷ 6 = 3	15 ÷ 3 = 5	18 ÷ 2 = 9	72 ÷ 8 = 9	21 ÷ 2 = 2
I.	30 ÷ 5 = 6	1 ÷ 1 = 1	21 ÷ 7 = 3	8 ÷ 4 = 2	0 ÷ 3 = 0
J.	9 ÷ 9 = 1	28 ÷ 4 = 7	16 ÷ 4 = 4	12 ÷ 2 = 6	36 ÷ 9 = 4
K.	8 ÷ 8 = 1	27 ÷ 3 = 9	6 ÷ 6 = 1	6 ÷ 3 = 2	0 ÷ 4 = 0
L.	12 ÷ 3 = 4	81 ÷ 9 = 9	0 ÷ 2 = 0	49 ÷ 7 = 7	36 ÷ 9 = 4
M.	40 ÷ 5 = 8	32 ÷ 8 = 4	9 ÷ 1 = 9	2 ÷ 2 = 1	14 ÷ 7 = 2
N.	35 ÷ 7 = 5	16 ÷ 2 = 8	0 ÷ 7 = 0	42 ÷ 6 = 7	6 ÷ 1 = 6
O.	45 ÷ 9 = 5	24 ÷ 4 = 6	10 ÷ 5 = 2	0 ÷ 1 = 0	12 ÷ 6 = 2
P.	2 ÷ 2 = 1	0 ÷ 5 = 0	24 ÷ 6 = 4	40 ÷ 5 = 8	24 ÷ 3 = 8
Q.	54 ÷ 6 = 9	27 ÷ 9 = 3	18 ÷ 3 = 6	25 ÷ 5 = 5	63 ÷ 9 = 7
R.	54 ÷ 8 = 8	63 ÷ 7 = 9	4 ÷ 4 = 1	0 ÷ 9 = 0	4 ÷ 2 = 2
S.	72 ÷ 8 = 9	63 ÷ 7 = 9	48 ÷ 8 = 6	27 ÷ 9 = 3	24 ÷ 8 = 3
T.	36 ÷ 4 = 9	54 ÷ 9 = 6	3 ÷ 3 = 1	40 ÷ 5 = 8	14 ÷ 7 = 2

Time: _____   Number correct: _____

101

Sentences & Fragments
Grammar

Read each group of words. If the group is only a fragment, write **F** on the line. If it is a sentence, write **S** on the line and add the correct ending punctuation. The first one has been done for you.

S 1. Isabelle is a good dancer .
F 2. To the park
F 3. Ride in the car
S 4. Be careful !
S 5. Stacey liked the movie .
S 6. Will you come over tomorrow ?
F 7. On top of the house by the chimney
F 8. With Tina and Gina

Division Designs

Divide. Then connect the dots in order, beginning with the number given first.

Start at 6

A. 30 ÷ **5** = 6   F. 56 ÷ **7** = 8
B. 15 ÷ **3** = 5   G. 6 ÷ **6** = 1
C. 28 ÷ **7** = 4   H. 21 ÷ **3** = 7
D. 20 ÷ **5** = 4   I. 40 ÷ **8** = 5
E. 9 ÷ **1** = 9   J. 48 ÷ **6** = 8

Start at 2

A. 5 ÷ **1** = 5   G. 45 ÷ **5** = 9
B. 63 ÷ **7** = 9   H. 12 ÷ **3** = 4
C. 9 ÷ **3** = 3   I. 21 ÷ **7** = 3
D. 8 ÷ **2** = 4   J. 63 ÷ **9** = 7
E. 18 ÷ **6** = 3   K. 25 ÷ **5** = 5
F. 56 ÷ **8** = 7

102

Complete Subjects
Grammar

Draw a line under the **complete subject** of each sentence below.

1. Astronauts are very brave people.
2. Donna's birthday is today.
3. The big, red boat sped across the water.
4. The spectators enjoyed the fireworks.
5. Barbara and Cindy love to garden.
6. The blue engine stopped at the station.
7. The actor was excellent in the play.
8. The movie was the best one I have ever seen!
9. Good health is important to everyone.
10. All children love to play.
11. The pictures in that book are beautiful.
12. The raft floated across the lake.

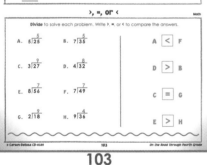

>, =, or <
Math

Divide to solve each problem. Write >, =, or < to compare the answers.

A. 5)25 = 5   B. 7)35 = 5   A **<** F

C. 3)27 = 9   D. 4)32 = 8   D **>** B

E. 8)56 = 7   F. 7)49 = 7   C **=** G

G. 2)18 = 9   H. 9)36 = 4   E **>** H

103

Division Practice
Math

Divide to solve each problem.

A. 4)24 = 6   A. 9)72 = 8   C. 4)36 = 9   D. 7)70 = 10

E. 2)12 = 6   F. 4)16 = 4

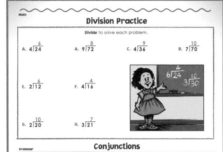

G. 2)20 = 10   H. 3)21 = 7

Conjunctions
Grammar

Select the correct **conjunction** to complete each sentence. Write it on the line.

and   but   or

1. I have enough money to buy both a ball **and** a bat.
2. You may have either milk **or** juice to drink.
3. Her favorite sandwich is peanut butter **and** jelly.
4. John took swimming lessons, **but** he still could not swim.
5. Mom said I can choose either pancakes **or** waffles.
6. We will go either to the mountains **or** the ocean on our vacation.
7. The United States' flag is red, white, **and** blue.
8. Johnny worked very hard on his report, **but** he only made a B.

104

Understanding What I've Read
Reading Comprehension

Independence Day

The Fourth of July is an important holiday for the United States. It is Independence Day. On July 4, 1776, the United States declared, or stated, that it was a country. It would no longer be part of England. "Independence" means to take care of yourself without help from others. That is why July 4 is called Independence Day. Every Fourth of July people in the United States celebrate the beginning of the country. There are parades, speeches, and lots of fireworks. People fly their flags to show they are proud of their country.

1. What is the main idea of this story?
   (a.) The founding of the United States is celebrated on July 4.
   b. Parades are common on July 4.
   c. July 4 is for fireworks.

2. On what day does the United States celebrate its independence?
   July 4

3. What word means to **state or say**?
   (a.) declare
   b. celebrate
   c. fireworks

4. What are some ways people celebrate Independence Day?
   parades, speeches, fireworks, waving flags

5. From whom did the United States declare its independence?
   England

6. What does the word **independent** mean?
   a. holiday
   b. stated
   (c.) free and on your own

105

Division
Math

Divide to solve each problem.

A. 56 ÷ 7 = **8**   B. 24 ÷ 8 = **3**   C. 54 ÷ 9 = **6**

D. 32 ÷ 8 = **4**   E. 12 ÷ 3 = **4**   F. 25 ÷ 5 = **5**

G. 50 ÷ 5 = **10**   H. 42 ÷ 7 = **6**   I. 72 ÷ 9 = **8**

J. 66 ÷ 6 = **11**   K. 40 ÷ 5 = **8**   L. 21 ÷ 3 = **7**

Main Idea
Reading Comprehension

The **main idea** of a paragraph is its central thought or topic. Read each paragraph and the three phrases below it. Decide which one tells the main idea. Write the letter of that phrase on the line.

a 1. Taffy's little brother was missing again. At least, no one knew where he was. Little Jeff could get into the strangest places. He would stay hidden until everyone was worried or mad. His favorite place to hide was in the clothes hamper. Taffy's mother said they should put a bell on Jeff!
   a. A mischievous boy   b. The clothes hamper   c. Taffy's family

b 2. Waterskiing is a lot of fun once you learn how. Sailing and boating are nice ways to spend a summer day. Water polo is fun to play. If you are near the ocean, bodysurfing and windsurfing are really exciting.
   a. Summertime   b. Water sports   c. Waterskiing

c 3. Ted asked his dad if he could have an allowance. Ted's dad said that he certainly could! He also said that Ted would have to do a few chores around the house. That was how he would earn his allowance. Every week Ted had to mow the lawn. He also had to take out the garbage. Ted had only been earning an allowance for three weeks. He was already thinking of asking for a raise!
   a. Cleaning the garage   b. Ted and his dad   c. Earning an allowance

106

Writing Sentences
Grammar

Read each pair of sentences. Rewrite the facts in a single sentence on the line.

1. Anna went to the beach. Anna wore her new bathing suit.
   Sentences will vary.
2. Billy hit a home run. Billy's team voted him the player of the game.
3. Charlie fell down the steps. Charlie was embarrassed.
4. Dianne went to the mall. Dianne bought a pair of jeans.
5. Eric painted a picture. Eric got paint on the floor.
6. Fran went to Gina's house. Fran and Gina played games.

Division Facts
Math

Divide to solve each problem.

A. 63 ÷ 9 = **7**   B. 49 ÷ 7 = **7**   C. 15 ÷ 3 = **5**

D. 64 ÷ 8 = **8**   E. 30 ÷ 6 = **5**   F. 80 ÷ 8 = **10**

G. 12 ÷ 2 = **6**   H. 45 ÷ 5 = **9**   I. 81 ÷ 9 = **9**

107

Magic Trail
Math

Follow the trail by solving the math problems. Can you find the magic number?

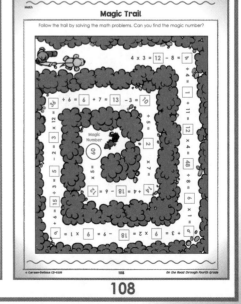

108

Answer Key

Division with Remainders

Divide to solve each problem.

A. $7\overline{)52}$ = 7 R3 B. $9\overline{)83}$ = 9 R2 C. $6\overline{)40}$ = 6 R4 D. $5\overline{)29}$ = 5 R4

E. $9\overline{)42}$ = 4 R6 F. $3\overline{)55}$ = 18 R1 G. $5\overline{)27}$ = 5 R2 H. $2\overline{)37}$ = 18 R1

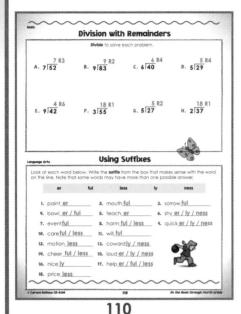

Using Suffixes

Look at each word below. Write the **suffix** from the box that makes sense with the word on the line. Note that some words may have more than one possible answer.

| er | ful | less | ly | ness |

1. paint _er_
2. mouth _ful_
3. sorrow _ful_
4. bowl _er / ful_
5. teach _er_
6. shy _er / ly / ness_
7. event _ful_
8. harm _ful / less_
9. quick _er / ly / ness_
10. care _ful / less_
11. will _ful_
12. motion _less_
13. coward _ly / ness_
14. cheer _ful / less_
15. loud _er / ly / ness_
16. nice _ly_
17. help _er / ful / less_
18. price _less_

110

Word Box Stories

Write eight words about the picture in the word box. Use the words to write a story. Be sure to use adjectives, capital letters, and periods. Give your story a title.

Things to Think About
Who is this story about?   Where does this story take place?
How does this story begin?   What happens next?
How will this story end?

Word Box

_____ Stories will vary. _____

111

Root Words

Look at each word below. Write each **root** word on the line.

1. nonsense — sense
2. rewrite — write
3. spoonful — spoon
4. happiness — happy
5. kindness — kind
6. brotherhood — brother
7. ticklish — tickle
8. quickly — quick
9. baker — bake
10. lovable — love
11. helpless — help
12. cleanness — clean

Three-Digit Dividends

Divide to solve each problem.

A. $5\overline{)125}$ = 25 B. $6\overline{)468}$ = 78 C. $4\overline{)632}$ = 158 D. $9\overline{)945}$ = 105

E. $8\overline{)704}$ = 88 F. $2\overline{)778}$ = 389 G. $7\overline{)672}$ = 96 H. $7\overline{)784}$ = 112

112

Predicates

The **simple predicate** is a verb that tells what the subject did or what was done to the subject. The **complete predicate** includes the verb and all the words that tell more about it.

Example: The white cat slept on the pillow.

The simple predicate is **slept** and the complete predicate is **slept on the pillow.**

Underline the complete predicate of each sentence. Circle the simple predicate.

1. Bess danced in the school play.
2. We went to the mall after the library.
3. California is a state on the West Coast.
4. The weather began to turn cool.
5. It rained for hours yesterday.
6. Opal made a painting for her mom.
7. Snow fell for six hours.
8. Seven students were in the spelling bee.
9. The tractor made a loud noise.
10. We served ice cream and cake at the party.

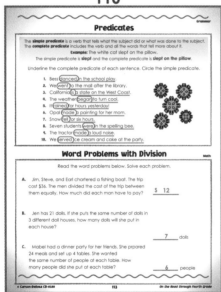

Word Problems with Division

Read the word problems below. Solve each problem.

A. Jim, Steve, and Earl chartered a fishing boat. The trip cost $36. The men divided the cost of the trip between them equally. How much did each man have to pay? $ 12

B. Jen has 21 dolls. If she puts the same number of dolls in 3 different doll houses, how many dolls will she put in each house?   7 dolls

C. Mabel had a dinner party for her friends. She prepared 24 meals and set up 4 tables. She wanted the same number of people at each table. How many people did she put at each table?   6 people

113

Main Idea

Circle or write the **main idea** of each paragraph.

1. It is September. It is the night of the first football game of the year. Everyone at Kidwell School is excited. Most excited of all is Cliff. This is the very first night he has ever marched with the band. He holds his clarinet nervously. As the director's white glove raises up, Cliff's heart skips a beat. He has dreamed of this moment and it is finally here. He is a member of the marching band.

   a. Cliff's first football game as a band member
   b. Excitement on the night of the first game
   c. Cliff and his friends at the football game

2. There are many different eyeglass frames. Some are very large. Some are simple and some are fancy. Carol liked every pair she chose. Her favorite pair looked like blue ovals.

   The main idea is: _Carol chooses eyeglass frames._

Money Word Problems

Divide to solve each word problem

A. Joe and Sam earned $24 raking leaves. They divided the money evenly between them. How much did each person get? $ 12

B. Mrs. Smith made 12 tacos. she gave her 4 children an equal number of tacos. How many tacos did each child receive?   3 tacos

C. Jamie and Eddie bought a pack of art paper. The pack contained 20 pieces of paper. If they each take the same amount of paper, how many pieces will they get?   10 pieces

D. Randi has a package of candy containing 49 pieces. If she wanted to eat an equal share of the candy every day for 7 days, how many pieces would she eat each day?   7 pieces

114

Identifying Misspelled Words

Underline the spelling error in each sentence. Write the correct spelling on the line.

1. Missy tripped while she was runing. — running
2. Do you beleeve that story? — believe
3. Valentine's Day is in Febuary. — February
4. I take gymnastics classes on Wensdays. — Wednesday
5. Mother made apple pie for desert. — dessert
6. I like to walk to scool. — school
7. Sara is going to the beech on Saturday. — beach
8. It is cool outside, so I will wear a sweter. — sweater

Adding Fractions

Add the fractions.

A. $\dfrac{5}{8} + \dfrac{2}{8} = \dfrac{7}{8}$ B. $\dfrac{4}{9} + \dfrac{3}{9} = \dfrac{7}{9}$ C. $\dfrac{9}{12} + \dfrac{1}{12} = \dfrac{10}{12}$ D. $\dfrac{1}{6} + \dfrac{4}{6} = \dfrac{5}{6}$

E. $\dfrac{2}{5} + \dfrac{3}{5} = 1$ F. $\dfrac{2}{4} + \dfrac{1}{4} = \dfrac{3}{4}$ G. $\dfrac{3}{5} + \dfrac{1}{5} = \dfrac{4}{5}$ H. $\dfrac{1}{6} + \dfrac{4}{6} = \dfrac{5}{6}$

119

Words into Math

Use the table to answer the questions.
If the information needed to answer a question is not given, write **NG.**

Daily Schedule	Time
Homeroom	8:00 – 8:10
1st Period	8:15 – 9:15
2nd Period	9:20 – 10:25
3rd Period	10:25 – 11:25
Lunch	11:25 – 12:00
4th Period	12:00 – 1:15
5th Period	1:05 – 2:05
6th Period	2:10 – 3:10

Charles High School has this daily schedule. It names all the class periods and gives the time each one starts and ends.

1. How long is each class period?   1 hour

2. If Jimmy gets to class at 8:30, how much of 1st period has he missed?   15 minutes

3. What class does Susan have 4th period?   NG

4. Kaitlin's mom picked her up at 2:00. During what period did she leave?   5th Period

5. Jamal stays in Mr. Wood's room for 2nd and 3rd periods. How long is he in that room?   2 hours

6. During what period does Ms. Smith teach gym?   NG

7. How long is the lunch period?   35 minutes

8. Which period begins at 9:20?   2nd Period

9. What event happens between 8:00 and 8:10 each morning?   Homeroom

10. If school is over after 6th period, what time do the students get out?   3:10

120

Division Facts 4–12 Review

Divide to solve each problem.

A. $9\overline{)90}$ = 10 B. $10\overline{)20}$ = 2 C. $11\overline{)99}$ = 9 D. $12\overline{)108}$ = 9 E. $11\overline{)77}$ = 7

F. $12\overline{)24}$ = 2 G. $10\overline{)60}$ = 6 H. $12\overline{)60}$ = 5 I. $11\overline{)110}$ = 10 J. $10\overline{)100}$ = 10

K. $9\overline{)27}$ = 3 L. $9\overline{)9}$ = 1 M. $10\overline{)120}$ = 12 N. $11\overline{)121}$ = 11 O. $9\overline{)108}$ = 12

Topic Sentence

A **topic sentence** is a sentence in a paragraph that tells the main idea.

Example: Ellen disliked all types of tiny, crawling things. Spiders made her crazy. Worms gave her the willies. Little, shiny lizards made Ellen feel awful. The only tiny, crawling thing Ellen liked was her little brother Ned.

Read each paragraph. Underline the topic sentence.

1. Raccoons sleep all day. They wake up at night to get food when they are hungry. Fireflies blink on and off at night. Owls hunt for their food after the sun goes down. Bats search for insects after dark. These are all night creatures.

2. There are many interesting things at the hairstyling shop. There is the stylist's chair that spins around and goes up and down. There are all the different combs, lotions, and special things the hair stylist uses. Some people like the magazines in the waiting area. Some folks like the hair styles they get the best!

3. The takeoff was surprisingly smooth. The sky was clear and there were only a few clouds. The flight attendants were all very friendly. Amanda thought her dinner on the plane was delicious. In fact, everything about Amanda's first airplane ride was perfect.

122

Math Puzzle

Solve the problems below and write the answers in the boxes. On the building, shade in the squares that match your answers. The answers will make a pattern.

5 × 3 – 6 = 9
27 ÷ 3 + 4 = 13
3 × 6 + 9 = 2
120 ÷ 10 × 11 = 132
32 ÷ 8 + 7 = 11
4 × 3 – 9 = 3
2 × 3 × 5 = 30
21 ÷ 7 + 4 = 7
81 ÷ 9 + 8 = 17
3 × 2 + 8 = 14
40 ÷ 5 + 8 = 16
56 ÷ 7 + 7 = 15
5 × 8 ÷ 10 = 4
4 × 9 ÷ 3 = 12
2 × 9 ÷ 3 = 6
33 ÷ 3 + 1 = 12

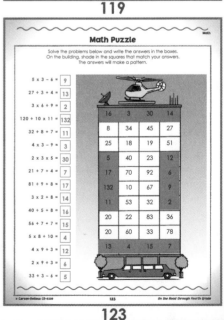

16	3	30	14
8	34	45	27
25	18	19	51
5	40	23	12
17	70	92	6
132	10	67	9
11	53	32	2
20	22	83	36
20	60	33	78
13	4	15	7

123

Answer Key

Page 125

Solve the Code

You must solve the code to find the alligator's name and cross the stream.
For each answer in the code, write the letter of the corresponding problem.

N	E	N	R	D
233 R1	116 R2	146 R2	304 R1	110 R4
4)933	8)930	5)732	3)913	9)994

M	A	S	H	W
163 R2	168 R4	413 R1	103 R2	114 R4
6)980	5)844	2)827	9)933	7)802

S	I	E	R	A
133 R3	167 R2	126 R3	122 R5	173 R2
7)934	3)503	6)759	8)981	4)694

H I S   N A M E
103 R4 304 R1 133 R3   233 R1 173 R2 163 R2 126 R3

I S
167 R2 413 R1

A N D R E W
168 R4 146 R2 110 R4 122 R5 116 R2 114 R4

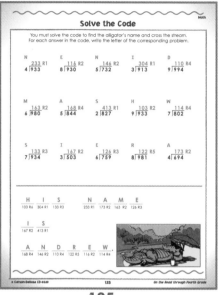

Page 126

Topic Sentence

A **topic sentence** is a sentence in a paragraph that tells the main idea.
Underline the topic sentence in each paragraph.

1. <u>Learning to play the piano was not always easy for Todd.</u> He did not always feel like practicing. Sometimes he made a lot of mistakes, even when he was trying hard. Some days, Todd would feel too tired to play. When Todd did start to get better, though, he was very proud.

2. Kim and Kurt spent $10 each for their stamp albums. Kim bought four special stamps from France. They cost $1 each. Kurt spent $6 on a set of Olympic stamps. <u>Collecting stamps was going to be expensive for the children!</u>

3. <u>Winters can be very hard in Vermont.</u> There are often heavy snowfalls with high winds. It can be days before some back roads are plowed. Many people in Vermont chop their own wood. That's very hard work. Many people drive special cars and trucks to get around on the snowy roads.

Adding Fractions

Add. Write each answer in simplest form. The first one has been done for you.

A. $\frac{2}{5} + \frac{1}{5} = \frac{3}{5}$ B. $\frac{3}{5} + \frac{1}{5} = \frac{4}{5}$

C. $\frac{7}{9} + \frac{1}{9} = \frac{8}{9}$ D. $\frac{1}{5} + \frac{2}{5} = \frac{3}{5}$

E. $\frac{3}{8} + \frac{4}{8} = \frac{7}{8}$ F. $\frac{5}{7} + \frac{1}{7} = \frac{6}{7}$

F. $\frac{1}{4} + \frac{3}{4} = 1$ G. $\frac{5}{6} + \frac{2}{6} = 1\frac{1}{6}$

Page 127

Fraction Addition

Add. Write each answer in simplest form. The first one has been done for you.

A. $\frac{1}{6} + \frac{1}{6} = \frac{1}{3}$ B. $\frac{3}{10} + \frac{1}{10} = \frac{2}{5}$

C. $\frac{1}{7} + \frac{3}{7} = \frac{4}{7}$ D. $\frac{6}{7} + \frac{3}{7} = 1\frac{2}{7}$

E. $\frac{1}{8} + \frac{3}{8} = \frac{1}{2}$ F. $\frac{2}{9} + \frac{5}{9} = \frac{7}{9}$

G. $\frac{5}{9} + \frac{1}{9} = \frac{2}{3}$ H. $\frac{2}{5} + \frac{3}{5} = 1$

Adjectives

Find and underline the **adjectives** in each paragraph.

1. Anna went to the <u>big</u> shoe store with her mother. Anna needed some <u>new</u> shoes. She saw <u>black</u>, shiny shoes and <u>white</u>, ruffled shoes. Anna especially liked the <u>fancy</u> <u>red</u> dress shoes with <u>black</u> and <u>white</u> trim. Anna decided to buy some <u>tan</u> shoes. Anna's mother paid the <u>tall</u> salesman, and Anna wore her <u>new</u> shoes home.

2. I like to watch the <u>brave</u> firefighters work. They wear <u>large</u>, protective outfits to keep them safe from fire. Firefighters try to save <u>small</u> houses, <u>big</u> houses, and <u>office</u> buildings. They will put out a fire anywhere. Sometimes, I have watched them put out fires in the <u>tall</u> forest behind my neighborhood. I would like to be a <u>brave</u> firefighter when I grow up.

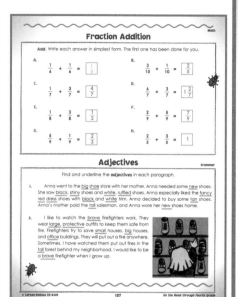

Page 128

Writing in the Third Person

This story is written from the first person **point of view**. Rewrite the story below, changing the point of view to third person. Add an ending to the story.

A Skating Disaster

I was skating on the sidewalk a few blocks from my house yesterday afternoon when a dog darted out of the bushes. The dog ran right across my path. Boom! Down I fell! I stood up and brushed myself off. Suddenly, a little boy out of the same bushes. The boy was calling, "Come back, Pixie!" As he rushed past me, I fell down again. I had just picked myself up again when a man raced out of the bushes! He was shouting, "Come back, Sergio! Come back, Pixie!" I . . .

Rosa was skating on the sidewalk a few blocks from her house yesterday afternoon when a dog darted out of the bushes. The dog ran right across her path. Boom! Down she fell! Rosa stood up and brushed herself off. Suddenly, a little boy ran out of the same bushes. The boy was calling, "Come back, Pixie!" As he rushed past Rosa, she fell down again. Rosa had just picked herself up again when a man raced out of the bushes! He was shouting, "Come back, Sergio! Come back, Pixie!" Rosa. . .

Stories will vary.

Page 129

Analogies

Compare the relationships of the words below.
Write a word on the line to complete each analogy.

1. car : driver :: plane : **pilot**
2. bird : sky :: fish : **ocean**
3. coffee : drink :: hamburger : **food**
4. small : tiny :: large : **huge**
5. glove : hand :: boot : **foot**
6. easy : simple :: hard : **difficult**
7. breakfast : lunch :: morning : **noon**
8. blue : color :: round : **shape**
9. date : calendar :: time : **clock**
10. win : lose :: stop : **go**

Subtracting Fractions

Subtract. Write each answer in simplest form. The first one has been done for you.

A. $\frac{2}{3} - \frac{1}{3} = \frac{1}{3}$ B. $\frac{7}{9} - \frac{5}{9} = \frac{2}{9}$

C. $\frac{3}{7} - \frac{1}{7} = \frac{2}{7}$ D. $\frac{3}{5} - \frac{1}{5} = \frac{2}{5}$

E. $\frac{5}{8} - \frac{2}{8} = \frac{3}{8}$ F. $\frac{3}{4} - \frac{1}{4} = \frac{1}{2}$

G. $\frac{8}{9} - \frac{3}{9} = \frac{5}{9}$ H. $\frac{4}{6} - \frac{2}{6} = \frac{1}{3}$

Page 130

Mixed Problem Puzzle

Solve the problems. Use the number key at the bottom of the page to color the picture.

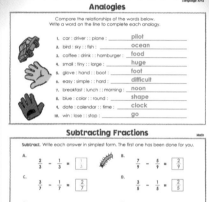

10 = yellow   16 = orange
15 = green   12 = purple

Page 131

Completing Analogies

Fill in the blanks to complete the **analogies**.

1. Ice is to **cold** as steam is to **heat**
2. The sun is to **daytime** as the moon is to **nighttime**
3. Perspiration is to **heat** as shivering is to **cold**
4. Birds are to **flying** as dolphins are to **swimming**
5. Books are to **reading** as radios are to **listening**
6. Shoes are to **feet** as gloves are to **hands**

Subtracting Fractions

Subtract the fractions. Write each answer in simplest form.

A. $\frac{6}{7} - \frac{2}{7} = \frac{4}{7}$ B. $\frac{6}{9} - \frac{3}{9} = \frac{1}{3}$ C. $\frac{9}{10} - \frac{5}{10} = \frac{2}{5}$ D. $\frac{6}{8} - \frac{2}{8} = \frac{3}{4}$

E. $\frac{3}{4} - \frac{1}{4} = \frac{1}{2}$ F. $\frac{2}{5} - \frac{1}{5} = \frac{1}{5}$ G. $\frac{8}{9} - \frac{7}{9} = \frac{1}{9}$ H. $\frac{2}{3} - \frac{1}{3} = \frac{1}{3}$

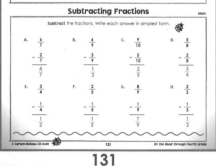

Page 132

Writing in the First Person

This story is written from the third person **point of view**. Rewrite the story, changing the point of view to first person. Add an ending to the story.

Soccer Hero

Joey has been playing soccer for three years. His team is called the Mountain Lions. Joey plays goalie on the team. A goalie tries to keep the other team from scoring by standing in front of the net and blocking any balls kicked toward it. Joey is a great goalie. He played on the All-Star Team last year. Last Thursday, the Mountain Lions played a team called the Blazing Suns. The Suns were ahead by two goals. The game was almost over and it looked like the Lions were going to lose. Joey . . .

I have been playing soccer for three years. My team is called the Mountain Lions. I play goalie on the team. A goalie tries to keep the other team from scoring by standing in front of the net and blocking any balls kicked toward it. I am a great goalie. I played on the All-Star Team last year. Last Thursday, the Mountain Lions played a team called the Blazing Suns. The Suns were ahead by two goals. The game was almost over and it looked like the Lions were going to lose. I . . .

Stories will vary.

Page 133

Proofreading

Circle each letter that should be capitalized.
Add punctuation marks in the proper places.
Write an ending to the story.

Creature from Outer Space

(T)im and (I) decided to camp out in the backyard.(W)e got our sleeping bags, two flashlights, and some snacks. (W)e unrolled our sleeping bags, lay down, and began to munch on some pretzels.(I)t was a clear night and the stars were sparkling brightly.(T)im found the (B)ig (D)ipper and the (N)orth (S)tar.(O)ne bright star seemed to be moving. (W)e watched it race across the sky.(S)uddenly, it stopped and began to grow bigger.(I)t was coming toward us.(I)t came to a stop right over our heads.(N)ow we could see that it was not a star at all.(I)t was a spaceship.(A) beam of light shot from the spaceship and glowed all around. (T)im . . .

Answer Key

Tic-Tac-Toe Synonyms

In each tic-tac-toe grid, circle three words in a row that are **synonyms**.

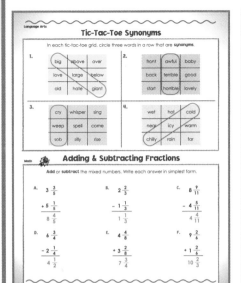

1.
big	above	over
love	large	below
old	hate	giant

2.
front	awful	baby
back	terrible	good
start	horrible	lovely

3.
cry	whisper	sing
weep	spell	come
sob	silly	rise

4.
wet	hot	cold
near	icy	warm
chilly	rain	far

Adding & Subtracting Fractions

Add or **subtract** the mixed numbers. Write each answer in simplest form.

A. $3\frac{3}{5} + 5\frac{1}{5} = 8\frac{4}{5}$

B. $2\frac{2}{3} - 1\frac{1}{3} = 1\frac{1}{3}$

C. $8\frac{9}{11} - 4\frac{5}{11} = 4\frac{4}{11}$

D. $6\frac{3}{4} - 2\frac{1}{4} = 4\frac{1}{2}$

E. $4\frac{4}{6} + 3\frac{2}{6} = 7\frac{3}{4}$

F. $9\frac{2}{6} + 1\frac{2}{6} = 10\frac{2}{3}$

134

Mixed Problems <, >, or =

Read each problem. Write the correct symbol (<, >, or =) on the line.

A. $60.5 > 60$

B. $6 \times 4 = 8 \times 3$

C. $3,345 < 4,002$

D. $95 > 93$

E. $72.5 > 72.1$

F. $40 \times 2 > 3 \times 30$

G. $145,092 < 147,958$

H. $\frac{8}{9} > \frac{7}{9}$

I. $50.3 > 50.2$

J. $97.05 < 97.50$

K. $\frac{12}{12} = \frac{8}{8}$

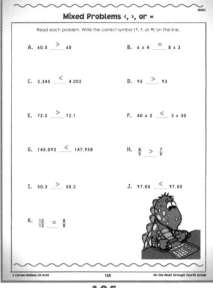

135

Words into Math

Read the story and answer the questions below.
If the information needed to answer a question is not given, write NG.

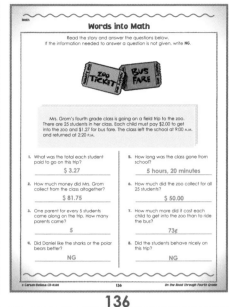

Mrs. Grom's fourth grade class is going on a field trip to the zoo. There are 25 students in her class. Each child must pay $2.00 to get into the zoo and $1.27 for bus fare. The class left the school at 9:00 A.M. and returned at 2:20 P.M.

1. What was the total each student paid to go on this trip? **$3.27**

2. How much money did Mrs. Grom collect from the class altogether? **$81.75**

3. One parent for every 5 students came along on the trip. How many parents came? **5**

4. Did Daniel like the sharks or the polar bears better? **NG**

5. How long was the class gone from school? **5 hours, 20 minutes**

6. How much did the zoo collect for all 25 students? **$50.00**

7. How much more did it cost each child to get into the zoo than to ride the bus? **73¢**

8. Did the students behave nicely on this trip? **NG**

136

Antonym Puzzle

Color the areas green that contain pairs of **antonyms**.
Color the rest of the design yellow.

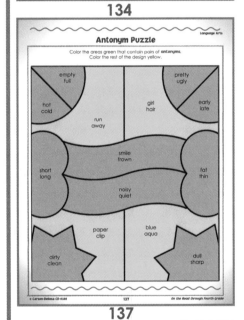

empty / full · pretty / ugly · hot / cold · girl / hair · early / late · run away · smile frown · short long · fat thin · noisy quiet · paper clip · blue aqua · dirty clean · dull sharp

137

Measure Sense

Using the chart, circle the measurement choice that is most reasonable.

STANDARD LENGTH
Inch (in.): the diameter of a quarter
Foot (ft.): from your shoulder to elbow
Yard (yd.): length of a teacher's desk
5,280 ft. = 1 mi.: a short car ride

A. length of a football field — **100 yd.** / 100 mi.

B. width of a math book — **8 in.** / 8 ft.

C. height of a fence — 4 in. / **4 ft.**

D. height of a desk — 2 in. / **2 ft.**

E. height of a doorway — 7 in. / **7 ft.**

F. width of your wrist — **3 in.** / 3 ft.

G. length of a parking lot — **50 yd.** / 50 mi.

H. length of your foot — **7 in.** / 7 ft.

Conversion Excursion

Use the conversion chart to complete the statements below.

Standard Length	
12 in.	= 1 ft.
3 ft.	= 1 yd.
5,280 ft.	= 1 mi.
1,760 yd.	= 1 mi.

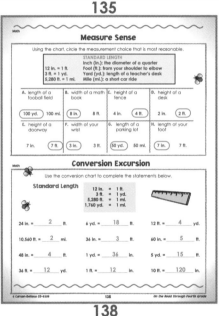

24 in. = **2** ft.

6 yd. = **18** ft.

12 ft. = **4** yd.

10,560 ft. = **2** mi.

36 in. = **3** ft.

60 in. = **5** ft.

48 in. = **4** ft.

1 yd. = **36** in.

5 yd. = **15** ft.

36 ft. = **12** yd.

1 ft. = **12** in.

10 ft. = **120** in.

138

Spelling Assessment

Read each group of words. Mark the word that is **not** spelled correctly.

1. several / skirt / spirel / strain / torn
2. yawn / yourselves / wow / wastte / twin
3. tomato / sword / stole / sparkel / sixth
4. serve / ruber / rear / prepare / pinch
5. pad / neklace / mess / knife / hero
6. footprint / ten / dozzen / degree / create
7. coast / cellar / broom / behav / attention
8. gloom / footstep / envelope / drag / creeture
9. cent / belly / attick / address / account
10. avenue / bufalo / colorful / croak / dentist
11. dredful / event / fifty / forward / goodbye
12. guy / history / ink / lace / lawwer
13. pale / sadie / shady / slam / stray
14. guy / tough / underground / waremth / fin
15. mist / nibble / place / pitcker / princess
16. rust / skunk / spit / fame / yesterday
17. warn / twice / tip / stirr / slip
18. rowboat / readder / pill / package / neat
19. merry / lood / herd / guide / glitter
20. ache / awakken / birdhouse / buggy / charm
21. comb / crocoodile / department / examine / gym
22. actual / acorn / aim / awerd / birth
23. chatter / comfort / crooke / depend / drift
24. example / fought / haircut / inssist / laid
25. lung / mister / noble / plannet / sadness
26. shogy / slant / split / tangle / tour
27. sort / single / September / ray / lizard
28. helpless / geust / glide / football / female

143

Narrative Passage

Read the story, then read each question. Read all the answers and mark the space for the answer you think is right. Mark NH (not here) if the answer can not be figured out from the given information.

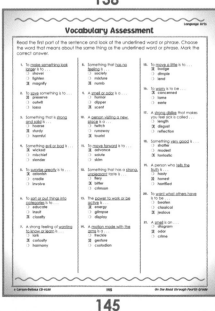

Lillian slid lower in her chair. She was almost under her desk. If she could just disappear, maybe the teacher wouldn't call on her. Lillian was prepared. She loved to read and had finished the book two weeks ago. She also liked to write, so the book report was no problem. Lillian did not want to read her report to the class. Her stomach felt sick and her face got hot every time she thought about standing up in front of all those children. The teacher called Lillian's name. Lillian slowly stood up and shuffled to the front of the room. She thought about Sam, a character in her book. If only she could be as brave as he was. Suddenly, Lillian knew what to do! She closed her eyes and pretended she was Sam. She told Sam's story, just as if it had happened to her. When she was finished, Lillian opened her eyes and looked at the class in front of her. They were clapping wildly because she had given such a good report! The teacher was very happy and gave Lillian an A+ on her report. Lillian was happy, too!

1. Why was Lillian trying to hide under her desk?
   - **She did not want to give the report.**
   - She was not feeling well.
   - She always hid under there.
   - NH

2. Lillian was afraid of something. What was she afraid of?
   - reading aloud
   - **standing up in front of the class**
   - her teacher
   - NH

3. Why did the teacher make Lillian give the report?
   - She didn't like Lillian.
   - It was Lillian's turn to report.
   - **She wanted Lillian to be brave.**

4. How did Lillian help herself get through the report?
   - She pretended she was at home.
   - She pretended to be brave.
   - **She pretended to be Sam.**
   - NH

5. What words from the story give clues about how Lillian felt giving book reports in front of the class?
   - brave, pretended, wildly
   - happy, character, problem
   - **disappear, sick, shuffled**

6. What grade did Lillian get for her report?
   - **A+**
   - E+
   - A
   - NH

144

Vocabulary Assessment

Read the first part of the sentence and look at the underlined word or phrase. Choose the word that means about the same thing as the underlined word or phrase. Mark the correct answer.

1. To make something look larger is to . . .
   - shovel
   - tighten
   - **magnify**

2. To save something is to . . .
   - **preserve**
   - outwit
   - lasso

3. Something that is strong and solid is . . .
   - hoarse
   - **sturdy**
   - harmful

4. To surprise greatly is to . . .
   - **astonish**
   - cradle
   - involve

5. To sort or put things into categories is to . . .
   - educate
   - insult
   - **classify**

6. A strong feeling of wanting to know or learn is . . .
   - lark
   - **curiosity**
   - harmony

7. Something that has no feeling is . . .
   - society
   - mixture
   - **numb**

8. A smell or odor is a . . .
   - humor
   - dipper
   - **scent**

9. A person visiting a new place is a . . .
   - twitch
   - runaway
   - **tourist**

10. Something evil or bad is . . .
   - **wicked**
   - advance
   - salute

11. To move forward is to . . .
   - **advance**
   - salute
   - skim

12. Something that has a strong, unpleasant taste is . . .
   - fiery
   - **bitter**
   - crimson

13. The power to work or be active is . . .
   - **energy**
   - glimpse
   - display

14. A motion made with the arms is a . . .
   - freckle
   - **gesture**
   - custodian

15. To move a little is to . . .
   - **budge**
   - dimple
   - lend

16. To worry is to be . . .
   - **concerned**
   - lame
   - eerie

17. A strong dislike that makes you feel sick is called . . .
   - length
   - **disgust**
   - reflection

18. Something very good is . . .
   - shatter
   - modest
   - **fantastic**

19. A person who tells the truth is . . .
   - hasty
   - **honest**
   - horrified

20. To want what others have is to be . . .
   - beaten
   - classical
   - **jealous**

21. A smell is an . . .
   - diagram
   - **odor**
   - crime

145

Place Value with Large Numbers

Use the given number to find the place values. The first one has been done for you.

1. The number is: **7,320,149.685**
   a. Name the digit in the tens place. **4**
   b. Name the digit in the tenths place. **6**
   c. Name the digit in the millions place. **7**
   d. Name the digit in the ones place. **4**
   e. In what place value is the digit 0? **thousands**
   f. In what place is the digit 2? **ten thousands**
   g. In what place value is the digit 3? **hundred thousands**
   h. In what place value is the digit 5? **thousandths**

2. The number is: **8,635.147**
   a. Name the digit in the hundreds place. **6**
   b. Name the digit in the hundredths place. **4**
   c. Name the digit in the thousands place. **8**
   d. Name the digit in the tenths place. **1**
   e. Name the number that is one hundred more. **8,735.147**
   f. Name the number that is one thousand less. **7,635.147**
   g. Name the number that is one-hundredth less. **8,635.137**
   h. Name the number that is one more. **8,636.147**

3. The number is: **1,320,796.485**
   a. Name the digit in the millions place. **1**
   b. Name the digit in the ones place. **6**
   c. Name the digit in the thousandths place. **5**
   d. Name the digit in the ten thousands place. **2**
   e. Name the number that is ten thousand less. **1,310,796.485**
   f. Name the number that is one-thousandth more. **1,320,796.486**
   g. Name the number that is one less. **1,320,795.485**
   h. Name the number that is one million more. **2,320,796.485**

146

Cut-and-Color Awards

I understand analogies!

Name: _____ Date: _____

I can multiply LARGE numbers!

Name: _____ Date: _____

I can identify the topic sentence in a paragraph!

Name: _____ Date: _____

I know my math facts!

Name: _____ Date: _____

I can divide LARGE numbers!

Name: _____ Date: _____

nouns   verbs   adverbs

I know my parts of speech!

adjectives

Name: _____ Date: _____

I can use punctuation correctly!

Name: _____ Date: _____

I understand synonyms, homonyms, and antonyms!

Name: _____ Date: _____